NATURAL ENVIRONMENT RESEARCH COUNCIL
INSTITUTE OF TERRESTRIAL ECOLOGY

ECOLOGICAL MAPPING FROM GROUND, AIR AND SPACE

ITE SYMPOSIUM NO 10

EDITED BY

R M FULLER

ITE, MONKS WOOD EXPERIMENTAL STATION,
ABBOTS RIPTON, HUNTINGDON

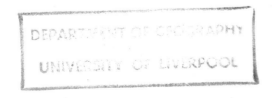
PROCEEDINGS OF A SYMPOSIUM HELD AT MONKS WOOD EXPERIMENTAL STATION
25-27 NOVEMBER 1981

Printed in Great Britain by NERC/SERC Reprographic Services, Swindon

First published in 1983 by Institute of Terrestrial Ecology
68 Hills Road
Cambridge
CB2 1LA
0223 (Cambridge) 69745

ISBN 0 904282 71 6
ISSN 0263-8614

ACKNOWLEDGEMENT

The figures were drawn with the assistance of Sarah Anthony and Andrew Foy.
Camera-ready copy was prepared by Mrs Barbara Stocker.

COVER PHOTOGRAPH

Four stages in the digital processing of a Landsat image of Cumbria.

TOP LEFT: A composite of 3 channels, 0.5-0.6 μm, 0.6-0.7 μm, 0.8-1.1 μm shown in blue, green and red respectively. The large area of red represents strong infrared reflectance from healthy vegetation.

TOP RIGHT: A colour composite presenting to the eye virtually all of the data in the 4 spectral channels. Red, green and blue in the image correspond to the first 3 principal components of the 4 channels.

BOTTOM LEFT: A scattergram of the second principal component against the first. For each point, the number of pixels having a particular combination of reflectance is represented by colour taken from the colour wedge: peaks correspond to different surface cover types. Histograms for the 2 components are shown around the edge.

BOTTOM RIGHT: An unsupervised classification of the data into 16 clusters; all points in the image having the same reflectance signature are in one cluster and are represented by a colour from the wedge.

For further details see Baker (this symposium).

The images were processed on the I^2S image analysis system and plotted on the Optronics colour filmwriter by R J Parsell at NERC Swindon.

The Institute of Terrestrial Ecology (ITE) was established in 1973, from the former Nature Conservancy's research stations and staff, joined later by the Institute of Tree Biology and the Culture Centre of Algae and Protozoa. ITE contributes to and draws upon the collective knowledge of the fourteen sister institutes which make up the *Natural Environment Research Council*, spanning all the environmental sciences.

The Institute studies the factors determining the structure, composition and processes of land and freshwater systems, and of individual plant and animal species. It is developing a sounder scientific basis for predicting and modelling environmental trends arising from natural or man-made change. The results of this research are available to those responsible for the protection, management and wise use of our natural resources.

One quarter of ITE's work is research commissioned by customers, such as the Nature Conservancy Council, who require information for wildlife conservation, the Department of Energy and the Department of the Environment, and the EEC. The remainder is fundamental research supported by NERC.

ITE's expertise is widely used by international organizations in overseas projects and programmes of research.

R M FULLER
Institute of Terrestrial Ecology
Monks Wood Experimental Station
Abbots Ripton
HUNTINGDON Cambridgeshire
PE17 2LS

04873 (Abbots Ripton) 381

CONTENTS

1 INTRODUCTION

F T LAST
Institute of Terrestrial Ecology, Bush Estate, Penicuik

I suspect that most readers of this volume will automatically assume that it is concerned with the mapping of plants and plant assemblages, possibly also touching upon the location of animals and features of topographical interest (mountains, bodies of freshwater whether static or flowing ....). But why shouldn't we also be concerned with the distribution of microbes when it is remembered that the assemblages of parasitic and non-parasitic microbes on plant surfaces (roots and leaves), ecosystems in miniature, are subject to the same natural laws as those more readily and more usually studied by ecologists. Because ecosystems, whether micro- or macro-, have features in common, and because the problems of mapping cryptogams will not be discussed elsewhere, I have decided to highlight some of the main issues of ecological mapping by discussing the distribution, around trees, of toadstools produced by fungi that form sheathing (ecto-) mycorrhizas.

Over the years, I have enjoyed being involved, at one and the same time, with the unstructured approach at weekends of fungus forays, and with the more disciplined attitudes of quantitative microbial ecology on weekdays. However, bearing in mind the effort expended when searching for, and identifying, toadstools associated with trees, a simple statement that x species of fungi were found in a birch woodland - the typical summary of a fungus foray - is, for me, a totally unrewarding outcome. Couldn't something more ecologically worthwhile have been achieved? In 1977, my colleagues and I counted and identified 19 096 toadstools, noting, at the same time, that they were associated with 60 birch (*Betula* spp.) trees in an area of 540 m^2 or 0.054 ha. Thus, with the minimum of additional information, we were able to extend the value of our observations: we were able to quote the occurrence of fruitbodies as numbers per tree (320) or numbers per ha (350 000) (Mason *et al.* 1982).

Even to the uninitiated, it should be perfectly obvious that toadstools are not produced at random (Figure 1). By taking the co-ordinates of every

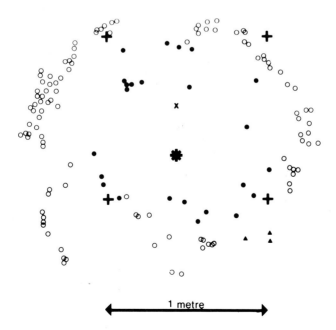

1 metre

*Figure 1   Distribution of fruitbodies of sheathing mycorrhizal fungi in 1977 around one of 60 birch trees (✱) (*Betula pendula*) growing at Bush Estate near Edinburgh. (The tree was planted, with others, in 1971)*

    O Hebeloma;   ● Lactarius;   × Leccinum;   ▲ Ramaria

toadstool, it soon became possible, with the help of an appropriate computer program, to show that toadstools of different fungi occupy different spaces. While there were differences from tree to tree, *Hebeloma*, *Inocybe*, *Laccaria* and *Lactarius* were usually the most abundant genera, with toadstools of *Hebeloma crustuliniforme*, poison pie, being concentrated in a concentric zone at a distance of 1 m (radius) from replicate birch trees, whereas those of *Lactarius pubescens* were densest at a radius of 640 mm. In contrast, *Inocybe lanuginella* toadstools, like those of *Laccaria*, were more or less equally densely distributed (numbers m^{-2}) except at the periphery of the laterally spreading system of roots. Thus, by taking co-ordinates, it was possible to record and characterize two different patterns of distribution, one of which was subdivided as a result of subsequent analyses. Whereas the toadstools of *Inocybe lanuginella* were randomly distributed within concentric annuli (zones), those of *Laccaria* were conspicuously aggregated to form linear patterns, probably paralleling the environs of secondarily thickened roots which, unlike most roots which become mycorrhizal, are not ephemeral.

At this stage, I would like to summarize what has been achieved. By adding *details of habitat*, in this instance 'numbers of trees' and 'areas occupied' (in other circumstances, details of ground vegetation, soil type, etc, may be added or substituted), the value of the toadstool observations was greatly enhanced - the exercise has become infinitely more rewarding with increased *time-effectiveness*, a major consideration. By punctiliously recording co-ordinates, distributions which are not always obvious to the eye can be identified if the data are held in a form facilitating subsequent analyses. Nowadays, this implies *computer-compatibility*, a desirable objective which can be readily achieved if *data collection* is arranged correctly from the outset.

As I will indicate later, much more needs to be known about pattern, and its analysis, an area of weakness in ecological understanding. I should also draw attention to statistical aspects because I would wish to challenge the need for many of the complete enumerations beloved by conservationists and ecological mappers, among whom I include physical planners.

As it happens, the 60 birch trees already referred to include specimens of silver birch (*B. pendula*) and downy birch (*B. pubescens*) grown from seeds collected at latitudes ranging from 50°N to 66°N. While specimens of *B. pendula* and *B. pubescens* had similar mean numbers of toadstools, appreciably more species of fungi were associated with the former (20) than with the latter (16). Further, and totally unexpectedly, an average of 50 toadstools was associated with trees from seed collected at 55°N but only 2.5 with those from seed collected at more northerly locations, latitude 66°N. This being so, shouldn't the team have taken notice of the benefits of *stratification*, not just as a result of hindsight? We started with 2 species of *Betula* and a range of seed collections made at latitudes sufficiently widely spaced to expect geno-typic differences - 'between' and 'within' species differences should have been used as *strata* from the inception of the project (Table 1). The discerning reader would be right to question the necessity to record and identify 19 000 toadstools. However, I have to admit, somewhat ashamedly, that the fungal survey which I have been describing developed like 'Topsy' - a poor way of implementing objective research. Essentially - I was incorrectly going to write ideally - I should have tackled the problems of stratification and subsampling at the outset to minimize the effort needed to acquire data of predetermined statistical reliability. As so often happens in biological research, the data were variable with standard errors increasing with increasingly large means, a statistical aspect having a profound influence on the choice of *transformation*, also of subsampling procedures. To some extent, I would justify some of the deficiencies that I have admitted. The 60 birch trees were planted to form a living gene-bank; they were not planted to enable a study of toadstool ecology. Fortunately, the replicate trees of each seedlot were arranged at random within the experi-

TABLE 1   Effects of seed collections (provenances) on numbers of toadstools
associated with *B. pendula* and *B. pubescens* grown at the same site
in Midlothian, Scotland (Mason *et al.* 1982)

| | | Numbers of toadstools per tree | | | | | |
| | 1975 | | 1976 | | | | |
Origin of seed	TOTAL	*Laccaria*	*Hebeloma*	*Inocybe*	*Lactarius*	TOTAL
I *Betula pendula*						
Lat. 57°N	219	76	287	11	10	384
Lat. 66°N	Nil	Nil	Nil	Nil	Nil	Nil
II *Betula pubescens*						
Lat. 52°N	231	23	359	Nil	15	397
Lat. 61°N	Nil	Nil	16	Nil	Nil	16

*seedlings transplanted to the field in November 1971

mental plot, and this design enabled the toadstool survey to be made without
fearing that differences were attributable to positional effects, as would have
been the case had replicate trees been grouped. Nevertheless, the experience
emphasizes the need to think and rethink the objectives of making a survey,
whether utilizing pencils and rulers or the most sophisticated forms of imagery.
Why is a particular survey being made? Are the data being abstracted in a way
that is generally useful? Do we need to have complete enumerations, or will a
reliable picture be obtained from much less effort directed in a more purpose-
ful manner, eg by following statistically correct sampling procedures?

While surveys, in themselves, are of value, their usefulness is often
greatly enhanced if they are made repeatedly, but at what frequency? With hindsight, I think we all regret the paucity, irregularity and very often incomplete-
ness of surveys made in the past, whether statistical surveys, the preparation
and revision of traditional maps, the procurement of aerial photographic records
(using fixed-wing aircraft or satellites). We have been slow to appreciate the
worth of monitoring, necessitating repeated surveys, and often suffer as a
result from an inability to reconcile the results of sequential surveys made
using different methods. We have regrettably deprived ourselves of the opportunity of learning as much as we should from past management changes. For the
future, I believe much more thought needs to be given to the ways in which our
environment, and changes in our environment, are recorded. However, without
considering how the potentially vast accumulations of data will be handled, this
exercise would be worthless. Why monitor? - a good question. For the last
time, I would like to revert to the plot of birches. As a result of sequential
surveys, it was found that the toadstools of the slower spreading *Lactarius
pubescens* were about the same mean distance from the trees in 1977 as were the
toadstools of the more rapidly spreading *Hebeloma crustuliniforme* 2 years
previously. By superimposing the relevant sets of data, a task aided by the
use of markers, it was found, not without surprise, that the spaces 'occupied'
by *L. pubescens* in 1977 were not those occupied by *H. crustuliniforme* in 1975
(Ford *et al.* 1980). The superimposed distributions suggest that there is a
very considerable degree of mutual exclusion between the 2 fungi, a feature
of their ecology that was not foreseen. How many other exciting and totally
unexpected phenomena will be revealed by monitoring? We tend to forget that

ecosystems, both micro- and macro-, are dynamic. Their components are constantly changing, but our methods of surveying must retain a degree of constancy, whether using simple and often disarmingly effective methods, or resorting to the excitements of sometimes ill-considered sophistication.

But, irrespective of method, I would, in summary, stress the virtues of:

1.   enumerating objectives,

2.   attempting to be time-effective: consider the benefits to be obtained from statistical procedures, subsampling by strata (stratification), enabling confidence limits to be calculated in a rational manner,

3.   making repeated compatible surveys so as to assess temporal and spatial changes,

and, finally,

4.   ensuring that data are collected in a form, in most instances computer compatible, that facilitates their subsequent analysis.

We are not here to decide "Which is the best technique?" Instead we should aim to learn the strengths and weaknesses of a variety of techniques so as to be in a position to match them against the requirements of our objectives.

REFERENCES

FORD, E.D., MASON, P.A. & PELHAM, J. 1980. Spatial patterns of sporophore distribution around a young birch tree in three successive years. *Trans. Br. mycol. Soc.*, 75, 287-296.

MASON, P.A., LAST, F.T., PELHAM, J. & INGLEBY, K. 1982. Ecology of some fungi associated with an ageing stand of birches (*Betula pendula* and *B. pubescens*). *For. Ecol. & Manage.*, 4, 19-39.

II STATISTICAL CONSIDERATIONS

STRATEGY FOR SUCCESSFUL SURVEY

K H LAKHANI

Institute of Terrestrial Ecology, Monks Wood Experimental Station, Huntingdon

ABSTRACT

The scientist engaged on an observational programme should seek to obtain the maximum amount of relevant information for minimum cost. The conclusions should be clear and precise, and seen to be based on acceptable scientific method. Thus, the scientist should be familiar not only with the observational material but also with the essentials of sampling techniques, experimental designs and statistical methodology. The literature in these areas is extensive and growing, requiring a close collaboration between the scientist and the statistician. This paper gives an introduction to the main steps underlying a survey.

INTRODUCTION

Our knowledge, opinions and attitudes are based on our limited experience and interactions with other people and events. Events in nature - the very phenomena of birth, of living and experiencing, even death - are the results of complex sampling processes. In everyday life, the many decisions that we make are based on samples of past experience.

What is true in everyday life is equally true in scientific investigations. Quite a lot of the complex interactions occurring in nature might be intrinsically uncertain and beyond our myopic comprehension. Even if the universe was deterministic, we have neither the ability nor the resources to assess, with complete precision, all relevant particular considerations; and we find ourselves forced to describe and explain from a limited amount of information.

In any given study, the extent of our success depends upon the nature of the population being studied, the variable of interest, the sampling design and the size of the sample, the accuracy of the measuring methods, and the appropriateness and the adequacy of the mathematical and analytical methodology used. The scientist, engaged to carry out a survey, is thus placed in an almost impossible position: not only must he have expert biological and ecological knowlege of the nature of the observational material, he must also have a detailed understanding of the subject of the design and analysis of experiments, and also of the sampling methods for censuses and surveys. There are, of course, many text books on these subjects: a selected sample is listed at the end of this paper. However, the text books tend to be highly technical. For most scientists, an optimum policy is, perhaps, not to attempt to master the books, but to gain familiarity with the basic concepts underlying the subjects of sampling methods and experimental designs, and, then, to seek out a friendly statistician who is interested in the scientist's problems, and who is willing to act collaboratively and collectively with the scientist.

ESSENTIAL CONSIDERATIONS FOR A SUCCESSFUL SURVEY

It is obviously naive to suppose that it is possible to provide, in so short a paper as this one, a comprehensive guide to the principles of statistical methods and sampling design. This does not preclude, however, the presentation of a brief account, highlighting the importance of some of the considerations. Thus, a good summary of the basic principles is given in the first 64 pages of Green's (1979) book *Sampling design and statistical methods for environmental biologists*. The statistical checklists by Jeffers (1978 & 1979) on *Design of experiments* and on *Sampling* cover only a few pages, but succeed in getting across to biologists and statisticians alike the important questions which must be taken into account in the application of statistical and sampling methods to practical research. The present paper discusses a number of features which are common to most investigations (see Cochran 1963). In organizing a new survey, the scientist should consider carefully the following features.

Objectives

It is essential that the objectives of the survey are clearly defined and well known to all staff participating in the study. If this is not done, it is very easy, during the later stages of planning or measuring or analysing, to make decisions which do not quite agree with the objectives. The degree to which the investigation succeeds depends, of course, on how one measures success, but an obvious criterion is to assess the degree to which the specified objectives were attained. An additional advantage of clearly set out objectives is that their very existence presents a challenge to the team of workers to direct their collective creative efforts towards the achievement of the aims of the exercise.

Population

The population which is being studied, and to which the conclusions from the survey will be applicable, must be clearly defined. The word *population* refers not to a biological population of the members of a given species, but to the complete collection of all individual entities of interest, eg the population of all books in a given library.

In an ecological mapping survey, the interest may be in the population of all non-overlapping quadrats, say 1 km^2, making up the study area. It is not always straightforward to identify clearly the collection of interest. Apart from boundary problems, there may be features within the study area (eg lakes, towns, railway lines, etc) which might be thought of as not belonging to the population. Even with a detailed definition, borderline cases are bound to arise, and it will be necessary to have clear rules enabling the field worker to decide, without much hesitation, whether or not the borderline case belongs to the population.

Since conclusions drawn from a sample apply only to the *sampled population*, it is necessary for the sample population to coincide with the *target population*, ie the population about which information is required. For example, a survey of the invertebrates of a given locality based on light trap catching methods may be misleading not only because the traps might succeed in catching invertebrates from other nearby localities, but also because the traps might fail to catch in appropriate proportions the different species which are in fact present, but are differentially active during the night. The extent to which conclusions from such a sample population apply to the target population must then depend upon other supplementary information which may not always be available readily.

Sampling units

Before the sample is selected, the population must be divided into parts called *sampling units*. For a biological population made up of all members of a given species, the sampling unit may be the individual member. Equally, the sampling unit may be a quadrat of a given size, the measurement of interest being, perhaps, the individuals found in a given quadrat. In a large scale mapping programme, the quadrat may be quite large, and the only practical measurement may be the recording of presence or absence of a given attribute.

Data

It is necessary to check that the data to be collected are *sufficient* and *relevant* for the objectives of the survey. A preliminary consideration of how the data will be analysed and presented may draw attention not only to the additional variables which must also be measured, but also to the possibility of discarding some of the variables which may be superfluous to the study.

Degree of accuracy

The results of the survey will be subject to some uncertainty because of the chance variation inherent in the sampling procedure and because of the errors of measurement. It is tempting, therefore, to increase the sample size and to improve the instruments and the procedures of measurement. These actions cost time and money. If the extent of error that can be tolerated is specified, it may be possible to recommend an economic sampling procedure, consistent with drawing reliable conclusions from the survey.

Sampling scheme

For most surveys there will be a number of ways in which the sample may be selected. To illustrate a few simple sampling schemes, we will suppose that the basic sampling unit is the 1 km^2 of the Ordnance Survey National Grid, and that the study area is made up of N such squares, numbered 1, 2, 3, ...,N.

Systematic sampling is obtained by randomly locating a grid of points over the study area. Such a scheme is convenient to use, and ensures that the sample points are well spread over the whole study area, but has a weakness that, if there is any periodicity in the population, and, if the sampling coincides with this periodicity, then the particular sample estimate may be grossly in error, and it will have a misleadingly small standard error.

A simple random sample gives each sampling unit the same chance of being included in the sample, regardless of which other units have already been selected. Given a population of N grid squares, a random sample can be obtained by drawing numbered tickets, which have been well mixed in a large hat, or by using a table of random numbers or by programming a computer to provide a random selection of numbers.

Relative to systematic sampling, simple random sampling requires greater care and work, but the advantage is that, if the data arising out of the mapping survey are used to estimate the population parameters of interest to the ecologist, the resulting sample estimates will be unbiased, and the calculated standard errors will not be misleading.

Stratified random sampling is the application of simple random sampling, not within the entire population of, say, N units, but separately within sub-populations of N_1, N_2, N_3, . . . etc, units. These subpopulations are non-overlapping and together they comprise the whole of the population, so that $N_1+N_2+N_3$ ...=N. These subpopulations are called *strata*, and it is important to bear in mind that, to obtain the full benefit from stratification, the subpopulation sizes N_1, N_2, N_3 . . . etc, must be known. There are a number of reasons why we may use *stratified random sampling*:

1.   We may simply wish to also obtain separate estimates for the different subdivisions of the population. This makes it necessary to treat the sub-divisions as if they were separate populations. Thus, a national survey of Great Britain may be subdivided into England, Wales and Scotland, or into other geographical or environmental regions.

2.   It may be convenient administratively to subdivide the population of interest. Thus, a national survey may be easier to conduct if the population is subdivided by regions or counties or other areas, with the regional staff carrying out the sampling locally. Care must be taken to provide, and enforce, adequate training for the active workers in the different regions. The train-ing should be centralised, and the field workers' performance should be assessed to verify that their observational ability is of uniform and comparable standard. If this is not done, it will be difficult to distinguish genuine differences between regions from spurious differences brought about as a result of regional differences in the expertise of the field workers from different regions.

3.   Stratification may improve the precision of the estimates. It may be possible to divide a heterogeneous population into strata (subpopulations), such that each stratum is reasonably homogeneous, in the sense that the measure-ments vary little from one unit to another within a stratum. Each stratum mean can then be estimated precisely from only a small sample in that stratum. The estimates for the different strata can be combined to obtain a precise estimate for the whole population. For example, in surveying the vegetation of a large area, it may be reasonable to suppose that, within each square, the values of the variables of interest would depend on the site characteristics such as rain-fall, altitude, soil types and slope. If so, before sampling begins, the popula-tion of grid squares should be stratified (ie classified) by these factors.

If stratification is based on, say, k *factors*, and if the ith factor has n_i levels, then the total number of strata will be the product of all the levels, n_1 x n_2 x n_3 x ... x n_k.

The theory of stratified sampling deals with the properties of the estimates from a stratified sample, and can be used to design the allocation of the sampling effort to different strata, so that the precision of the estimates will be maximized. Thus, the sampling effort to be allocated to a given stratum will be determined by the size of the stratum, the variability within the stratum and also on the cost of sampling, in terms of money or effort, within the stratum. The stratum variability and the cost of sampling in a stratum may not be known before sampling begins; but sampling can be controlled to take place sequentially, so that, for example, an initial allocation of a part of the total sampling effort may be made proportional to the stratum size, and the information on the variability and the cost of sampling within the strata, gained from the initial sampling effort, can be used to determine the allocation of the remaining sampling effort.

Apart from the 3 sampling schemes (systematic, simple random and stratified random), there are also other sampling designs (eg multi-stage sampling and cluster sampling) which are also frequently used. The sampling theory for surveys is mainly concerned about efficiently estimating the population parameters from the sample data.

Not all surveys are *analytical*, however, and, if the main objective of a survey is to produce a map or maps, then it can be argued that most of the sampling methodology in statistical literature is immaterial for achieving the goals of such a wholly descriptive survey. For ecological surveys, such an argument is short-sighted and unacceptable. Initially, the aim might well be to just describe. However, as soon as this phase is anywhere near completion, the ecologist would want to make comparisons between different subgroups of the population, with a view to discovering whether differences exist among them that may enable him to form or verify hypotheses about the processes at work in nature.

The recent advances in automatic recording techniques, and storage of almost unlimited amount of information on modern computer systems, together with our ability to tackle elaborate computational problems, mean that a purely descriptive ecological survey is now very much a thing of the past.

Methods of measurement

The sampling design defines the exact procedure to be followed for the selection of the sample units. Having identified a given sampling unit, it is obviously necessary to be clear as to what attributes or variables are to be measured or counted in each sample unit, and also how these measurements are to be made. A countable variable such as 'the number of plants in a quadrat' may present no difficulty if the individual plants are readily identifiable. On the other hand, the variable 'the number of earthworms in a quadrat' will generally mean not only the earthworms on the surface of the ground but also those underground. The numbers actually observed would then depend upon the extraction procedure used. The efficiency of the extraction procedure may itself depend on the earthworm activity which in turn may depend on variables such as soil temperature and soil moisture content.

Similarly, our ability to see and count other fauna will depend also on the size and colour of the fauna, and upon their mobility, abundance and behaviour. Data arising from pitfall traps, light-traps or suction sampling devices may not be easy to interpret. The green carpet of prevailing vegetation may produce ever-changing patterns through the seasons, and the insect species' variety and abundance may follow regular rhythms requiring great care in making decisions about the timing of field measurements.

Having made sure that the measurements are meaningful, relevant and adequate for the objectives of the survey, they need to be systematically recorded in a well-designed record form, which should be designed to also encourage the recording of unexpected occurrences in the field.

A pilot study

Unexpected occurrences always occur, and are, in a sense, expected. It is a good policy, therefore, to try out a preliminary field study on a small scale. This nearly always results in improvements in the record forms, may lead to modifications in the measuring methods, and may reveal other difficulties, such as a revised higher estimate of the total cost. Preliminary information, about the cost of sampling and relative variability in the different parts of the population, may provide a valuable basis for modifying the design of the sampling scheme, or the sampling allocation within the existing scheme.

Analysis of data

The type of analysis of the data will depend upon the procedure used for data collection, ie the sampling design and the method of measurement, the aim of the analysis being to achieve the objectives of the study. Preliminary arrangements for data handling on a suitable computer, including the development of routine computer programs, could be made before the sampling begins.

However, before rushing into any large scale 'number-crunching' exercise, it will be an advantage to discuss the analysis with an interested statistician, who should also be kept informed of the progress of the analysis. Statistical methodology is developing rapidly and continuously, and it is just possible that improved or alternative methodological techniques might have been publicized in the statistical literature since the initiation of the study. It is often the case that the proposed analysis of the observations requires that the data satisfy certain assumptions about the form of the distribution of the variables. The statistician, being aware of the assumptions, is often better placed to carry out initial checks of these assumptions, and, if necessary, to suggest appropriate transformations of the observations.

A preliminary examination may also indicate certain aspects of the data which may suggest modifications of the earlier decisions about the analysis. For example, it may be decided, after the data have been collected from a simple random sampling scheme, to carry out a stratification of the data. For example, in studying the rates of hedge removal from the interpretations of aerial photographs, Hooper (1968) classified his randomly selected study areas into arable, mixed and dairying farm types. Such a post-stratification amounts to correcting, to some extent, the earlier omission of not having foreseen the desirability of stratifying.

At times post-stratification may be even more efficient than stratification before sampling begins, because, after the sampling has been carried out, the stratification factors can be chosen in different ways, for different sets of variables, in order to maximize the gains in precision. This technique is particularly useful in multipurpose surveys where stratification factors selected before sampling may be poorly correlated with large numbers of secondary variables. Situations also arise where identifiable subgroups of the population do exist, but individual members can only be classified after sample selection. Thus, quadrats already observed may be classified by their soil pH measurements, but in practice this can only be done after the sample selection.

Presentation of results

The whole purpose of the statistical and numerical methodology is to isolate and describe the main trends and variations in the data, with a view to allowing and enabling the data to tell their own story. The results obtained, and also the data or their summary, need to be so presented that they leap to the eye. This condensation of detailed information into tables, graphs, charts and relationships is also part of statistical methods, and so, the statistician should be able to play a prominent part in the presentation of results.

Information gained for future surveys

A difficulty underlying the design of a sampling scheme for any population is that the choice of the scheme depends on the initial information we have about the population. As noted earlier, in stratified random sampling, the allocation of the sampling effort to different strata can be improved upon by an element of sequential sampling in the scheme. In the same way, it is obvious that any completed study is potentially a good guide for a similar future study. Thus, information about various estimates and their standard errors, and the cost of sampling in the earlier study, can be used to make judgements about sampling design, sample size and costs in a later study. In addition, a knowledge of the type of unexpected occurrences, and mistakes made in the earlier study are also of obvious value to the future worker. It is important, therefore, to assemble, record and make available all such information for future surveys.

GENERAL COMMENTS

1.   Unlike experiments, in which treatments are allocated to randomly selected plots and other variables are controlled as far as possible, the data arising from a survey are purely observational in nature, and require care and caution in analysis and interpretation. Thus, in an experiment, the observed differences may readily be attributed to the differences in treatments. On the other hand, in data arising from a survey, the observed differences in sampling units from different levels of a factor may well not be due to that particular factor, but to some other unknown but correlated factor.

2.   Care must also be exercised when the survey, perhaps because of its sheer size, is spread over a number of years. If different geographic regions are observed over different years, the apparent regional differences may well be due to the differential effects of the different calendar years on the variables of interest. In other words, using statistical language, the regional (spatial) effects may be *confounded* with the yearly (temporal) effects. A proper design would, of course, include a number of control units, to be observed each year. Such additional observations would be valuable to disentangle the regional effects from the yearly effects.

3.   Finally, it must be borne in mind that a survey, being a programme of observations at one time point, is like a single snapshot of nature. It will describe the status of the variables as measured at a given time point, and it will describe the prevailing relationships between different variables at the time of the survey; but, the survey will not, by itself, provide information on the rates of change in the values of the variables, in time.

CONCLUDING REMARKS

To summarize, ecological populations are complex, and their study requires great care and ability on the part of the scientist. Usually, it is neither possible nor wise to attempt to study the entire population. If the programme of observations is properly planned and conducted, the inductive approach of the statistical theory makes it possible to make probabilistic statements about the whole population, having observed only a part of it, a suitable sample of it.

To put it another way, nature does not yield her secrets readily – a price has to be paid in terms of manpower and resources. We would like to see and describe all of nature, in all her glorious and detailed contours and colours. This, alas, we cannot do. We can, however, have a peep at her, through the keyhole as it were, and, having seen a bit of her, create a complete image of her.

REFERENCES

COCHRAN, W.G. 1963. *Sampling techniques*. New York, London: Wiley.

GREEN, R.H. 1979. *Sampling design and statistical methods for environmental biologists*. New York: Wiley.

HOOPER, M.D. 1968. The rates of hedgerow removal. In: *Hedges and hedgerow trees*, edited by M.D. Hooper and M.W. Holdgate, 9-11. (Monks Wood Symposium no. 4). Abbots Ripton: Monks Wood Experimental Station.

JEFFERS, J.N.R. 1978. *Design of experiments*. (Statistical checklist 1). Cambridge: Institute of Terrestrial Ecology.

JEFFERS, J.N.R. 1979. *Sampling.* (Statistical checklist 2). Cambridge: Institute of Terrestrial Ecology.

SELECTED TEXT BOOKS

COCHRAN, W.G. & COX, G.M. 1950. *Experimental designs*. New York: Wiley.

COX, D.R. 1958. *Planning of experiments*. New York: Wiley.

FISHER, R.A. 1935. *The design of experiments*. Edinburgh: Oliver & Boyd.

SAMPFORD, M.R. 1962. *Introduction to sampling theory*. Edinburgh: Oliver & Boyd.

SCHEFFÉ, H. 1959. *The analysis of variance*. New York: Wiley.

SUKHATME, P.V. 1954. *Sampling theory of surveys with applications*. Iowa: Iowa State College Press.

YATES, F. 1960. *Sampling methods for censuses and surveys*. 3rd ed.. London: Griffin.

ANALYSIS OF SPATIAL DATA

J N R JEFFERS

Institute of Terrestrial Ecology, Merlewood Research Station, Grange-over-Sands

ABSTRACT

Methods of analysis of spatial data are defined partly by the design of the experiment or survey from which the data are derived and partly by the nature of the data themselves. A decision table for the type of analysis is suggested, together with a range of analysis techniques appropriate to various types of data.

INTRODUCTION

It is commonly assumed that the appropriate output of any scheme of ecological mapping from the ground, air or space is a map of some kind. Much of this symposium is, therefore, primarily concerned with problems of cartography, mapping or the presentation of spatial information in some graphical representation. However, the data from which such representations are derived may also be submitted to statistical analysis of various kinds, whether these data consist of attributes, categories or discrete or continuous variables. A further assumption seems to be that, where analysis is to be done, it will follow, rather than precede, the cartographic representation. In the worst of all possible cases, the analysis will actually be done on data derived from the cartographic representations themselves, rather than from the primary sources from which the cartographic presentation was itself derived. In this paper, I will challenge this assumption. It is my belief that analysis should precede cartographic representation, and that the analysis should be based on the primary data from which the cartographic representation is derived.

I do not want to dwell on the point, in this paper, but there are considerable dangers in the sheer sophistication of the techniques now available for the cartographic representation of spatial data. The principal danger is that of subjectivity. Given the enhanced flexibility of modern cartography, with its ability to stretch, tilt, colour and slice images, it is obvious that an infinity of combined images is now available to the well-trained cartographer. How does the cartographer select the final image from the infinity of possible combinations? Given the flexibility of modern instrumentation, it seems likely that he will manipulate the various elements until he achieves a representation which satisfies either his aesthetic taste or his preconceptions about the problem with which he is concerned. At this point, he may well cease any further experimentation with the variables that he is able to change in the representation. The resulting cartographic presentation may, therefore, be no more than a subjective expression of the cartographer's interpretation of the problem. What is more, even if this process is used to generate hypotheses, all of the data will already have been used in the generation of the hypothesis, thus leaving no 'new' data for the explicit testing of that hypothesis. Modern cartography does not, in this way, meet the criteria of the scientific philosophy by providing a falsifiable hypothesis. This is, of course, a somewhat extreme view of what cartographers do, and I have expressed it in this extreme way primarily to show the dangers of unequivocal acceptance of the sophistication which is available to modern technology.

A more important point about the use of cartographic information is that graphical and cartographic representation of spatial data frequently, if not inevitably, involves a disassociation between the objectives of the investigation, the methods by which the data were collected, and the methods by which those data are interpreted. As I shall emphasize later in the paper, the greatest dangers lie in this disassociation. The main message of my paper, therefore, is that analysis should always precede the cartographic presentation, and that the analysis should be defined by the objectives of the investigation, and by the method by which the data have been collected. Cartography and any form of visual presentation of spatial data would then be a secondary process, which necessarily follows analysis.

My assertion is dependent upon an important distinction between the 2 principal theories of data. Elsewhere (Jeffers 1981), I have emphasized that there are 2 quite distinct theories about the ways in which data can be used. First, there is what I call the 'accounting' theory of data which insists that data can be used in any way that seems appropriate to the user, in much the same way that records of transactions in company accounts are used to demonstrate various facets of the profitability, assets, and investment of a commercial or industrial company. The forms of presentation of such data take little or no account of the units in which the data were originally collected, the aggregations made at various stages in the accounting process, or the relationships of the data to other variables within the management and administration of the company. In contrast, the 'statistical' theory of data stresses the dependence of methods of analysis on the objectives of the investigation and the methods which were used to collect the data. These methods include such important points as sampling design, sampling units, definition of the attributes or variables collected within the investigation, and, particularly, the presence or absence of randomization, and any constraints that may have been placed on that randomization. Lakhani, earlier in this symposium, has already dealt with the essentials of sampling techniques, experimental designs and statistical methodology. Under this statistical theory of data, the kinds of analysis which can be made of spatial data are limited by the objectives of the investigation, and by the decisions made during the design and collection of the data. We may, therefore, make some considerable headway by a careful analysis of the strategies to be used in various kinds of environmental studies resulting in the collection of spatial data.

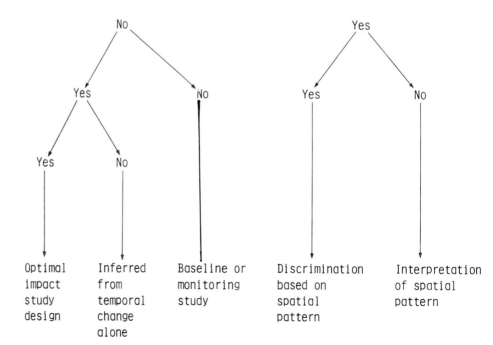

1. Has the 'impact' already occurred?

2. Is 'when and where' known?

3. Is there a control area?

Optimal impact study design

Inferred from temporal change alone

Baseline or monitoring study

Discrimination based on spatial pattern

Interpretation of spatial pattern

Figure 1   A decision key to determine the main strategies in studying environmental impacts (after Green 1979)

One of the most interesting classifications of the principal types of environmental study has been given by Green (1979) as a decision key related to the existence or non-existence of some 'impact', knowledge of when and where any such impact may have occurred, and the presence or absence of a control area. The main sequence of categories is given in Figure 1. From this Figure, it can be seen that the main strategies are determined quite simply by a sequence of yes/no answers to the 3 principal questions. If the 'impact' has already occurred, the principal division is made on whether or not the time and location of the impact occurrence is known. Similarly, if the impact has not occurred, and it is not known when or where such an impact is likely to occur, little more than baseline monitoring studies can be attempted. If the timing and place of the impact is known, then the determining factor is the presence or absence of a control area. In the paragraphs that follow, I will suggest methods of analysis for each of the 5 principal strategies defined by this simple decision table.

METHODS OF ANALYSIS

Interpretation of a spatial pattern

Where a supposed impact has already occurred, but it is not known when or where such an impact has taken place, the analysis is reduced to the interpretation of an existing spatial pattern. There are a large number of available techniques, but they can, broadly, be grouped into 3 categories, namely a) ordination, b) multidimensional scaling, c) cluster analysis. Ordination, or reification, is an attempt to attach some biological or physical meaning to mathematical expressions of spatial variation (Mather & Openshaw 1974). Techniques such as principal component analysis, factor analysis, principal coordinate analysis, reciprocal averaging, and indicator species analysis all have possible applications, but considerable skill and experience are necessary if any of the methods of analysis are to give a true picture of the physical meaning of the data. Indeed, if mathematical expressions of this sort have any obvious physical meaning, the result must be attributed to a lucky chance, or to the fact that the data have a strongly marked structure that shows up in the analysis. Even in the latter case, quite small sampling fluctuations can upset the interpretation (Harris 1975).

Multidimensional scaling is closely related to the techniques of ordination and has the aim of producing a visual representation with the smallest number of dimensions and which distorts the pattern of spatial representation as little as possible. In applications to spatial analysis, however, the technique is frequently based on a circular argument, the satisfactoriness of the representation being related to subjective interpretations of the displayed patterns. Perhaps the best known multidimensional scaling procedure is that of Sheppard, further developed by Kruskal (1964). The effectiveness of the method has been demonstrated by a remarkable reconstruction of the map of the departments of France by Kendall (1971). An entirely different technique (not involving multidimensional scaling) has since been devised by Kendall (1974) explicitly for the solution of problems such as this, which arise in a natural way in the context of historical geography. An earlier attempt was made by Geary (1954) through his development of the contiguity ratio.

Discrimination based on spatial patterns

The purpose of discriminant analysis is to investigate the relationship between a known grouping of data and the variables recorded (Harris 1975). The outcome of the analysis is an allocation rule, often, but not necessarily, associated with the values taken by a discriminant function. This rule can then be used for assigning to their appropriate groups the members of subsequent samples. With any allocation rule, there is associated a certain probability of miscalculation, and it is useful to be able to estimate this probability, at least roughly, and, of course, to choose the rule to make it as small as possible. The discriminant function is an extension of the linear models of the analysis of variance and of the multivariate analysis of variance, with a one-way classification. The disadvantage of the technique is that the statistical significance of the differences between the impact and non-impact areas is judged against variation within the areas. The absence of a control area precludes the possibility of a genuine error term in the analysis.

Baseline or monitoring studies

Baseline or monitoring studies precede the intended impact, and are intended to provide a base against which some future changes may be recorded. A wide range of techniques exist for such analyses, but one of the most popular, and, with some precautions, the most useful, is that of trend surface analysis (Unwin 1975). Provided that the appropriate mathematical functions are used to describe the trend surface, with adequate provision for discontinuities, the assumptions of this method are not too difficult to meet. The alternative method of automatic contouring, however, while apparently less demanding, has some extremely uncomfortable assumptions which are seldom justified in practical work. Nevertheless, automatic contouring remains a topic of great interest to mathematicians, an interest which is probably in inverse proportion to its applicability to real-life situations.

Impact inferred from temporal change alone

The absence of a control area in any spatial analysis which precedes the occurrence of a particular impact places severe constraints upon the kinds of analysis which can be undertaken. Typically, the analysis depends upon a comparison at 2 or more times spanning the period before and after the imposition of the change. Various methods of time series analysis are therefore appropriate, but the measure of experimental and survey error is inadequate because of the absence of the control (Findley 1978). An alternative approach is through the use of Markov models, where the transition probabilities before and after the introduction of change can be assessed (Collins *et al*. 1974). Such models are, however, somewhat restricted in their assumptions, although they have the advantage of a certain transparency in these assumptions.

Optimal impact study design

The optimal impact study design, where one or more control areas exist, allows for the use of 2-way analysis of variance or multiple analysis of variance. A wide range of possible models exist, depending upon the particular design of the control areas. In especially favourable conditions, the use of factorial designs is possible, thus enabling many factors to be studied, and to be separated from environmental variation not associated with the supposed impact.

Special problems

In the application of appropriate methods of analysis for the basic strategies of spatial analysis, there are some particular warnings to be heeded.

1.   Pay careful attention to the methods of sampling used in the collection of data. These methods will largely define the methods of analysis which are appropriate.

2.   The use of systematic sampling introduces special problems, particularly in the estimation of sampling errors.

3.   If random sampling has been used, make sure that any constraints placed on the randomization are known and understood, as they help to define the appropriate method of analysis.

4.   Be especially careful of data from a 'data bank', as these data will almost certainly have become disassociated from their methods of collection.

5.   It is not necessary to use all the data. Subsamples of the data set will provide a check on the repeatability of the results of the analysis.

6.   Check carefully any assumption made by the methods of analysis that you intend to use.

7.   Be especially cautious about using any method which is claimed to be 'the method'!

CONCLUSIONS

The analysis of spatial data follows closely the basic principles for the statistical analysis of any set of data, but has the added complication of the presence of spatial autocorrelation. Nevertheless, appropriate methods of analysis exist, and these are defined by the objectives of the investigation and by the methods used to collect the data. Three useful texts dealing with many of the problems touched on in this short paper are given by Cliff and Ord (1973) and Haggett *et al.* (1977a, b).

REFERENCES

CLIFF, A.D. & ORD, J.K. 1973. *Spatial autocorrelation*. London: Pion.

COLLINS, L., DREWETT, R. & FERGUSON, R. 1974. Markov models in geography. *Statistician*, 23, 179-210.

CORMACK, R.M. 1971. A review of classification. *Jl R. statist. Soc. A*, 134, 321-367.

FINDLEY, D.F. ed. 1978. *Applied time series analysis*. London: Academic Press.

GEARY, R.C. 1954. The contiguity ratio and statistical mapping. *Statistician*, 5, 115-145.

GREEN, R.H. 1979. *Sampling design and statistical methods for environmental biologists*. New York: Wiley.

HAGGETT, P., CLIFF, A.D. & FREY, A. 1977a. *Locational analysis in human geography. 1. Locational models*. London: Edward Arnold.

HAGGETT, P., CLIFF, A.D. & FREY, A. 1977b. *Locational analysis in human geography. 2. Locational methods*. London: Edward Arnold.

HARRIS, R.J.C. ed. 1975. *A primer of multivariate statistics*. London: Academic Press.

JEFFERS, J.N.R. 1981. The development of models in urban and regional planning. *Nature & Resour.*, 17, 14-19.

KENDALL, D.G. 1971. Construction of maps from "odd bits of information". *Nature, Lond.*, 231, 158-159.

KENDALL, D.G. 1974. Data-analytic problems in archaeology and history. *Proc. Euro. Meeting of Statisticians, 2nd, Budapest*.

KRUSKAL, J.B. 1964. Multidimensional scaling by optimizing goodness-of-fit to a non-metric hypothesis. *Psychometrika*, 29, 1-27.

MATHER, P.M. & OPENSHAW, S. 1974. Multivariate methods and geographical data. *Statistician*, 23, 283-308.

UNWIN, D. 1975. *An introduction to trend surface analysis*. (Concepts and techniques in modern geography no. 5). Norwich: Geo Abstracts.

III MAPS & ARCHIVAL DATA AS BASES FOR SURVEY

THE AVAILABILITY AND USE OF ARCHIVAL SOURCES OF INFORMATION

J SHEAIL
Institute of Terrestrial Ecology, Monks Wood Experimental Station, Huntingdon

ABSTRACT

The paper reviews the range of printed and manuscript sources of particular relevance to studies of the distribution and character of plant and animal communities in the past, with an emphasis on the earlier part of this century. The historical value of old maps and photographs, surveys of agriculture and woodlands, and the working papers and files of individuals and organizations is demonstrated.

INTRODUCTION

The ecologist frequently prefaces his study of a particular community or site with an historical review of how its present day composition and character developed. Such an approach is especially apposite where the subject of interest falls within a nature reserve, and where a knowledge of its former use and management may have a considerable bearing on deciding the most suitable forms of management for the future.

It was partly for this reason that the history of the site of Wicken Fen in Cambridgeshire excited so much interest. Since the 1890s, it has been managed by the National Trust as a nature reserve. Unfortunately, a close examination of the many attempts to reconstruct its history reveals them 'to be short on data, speculative, and divergent in their conclusions'. In his fresh study of the documentary sources on Wicken Fen, Rowell (1981) has made considerable use of hitherto unknown documents, and of the historian's deeper understanding of sources already known. Together with more recent observations on the topography and vegetation of the reserve area, a sounder basis may emerge for deciding a management policy. Many other sites of high ecological status would benefit from a reworking of their historiography. The last word will never be written on the history of any site or community.

SOURCES OF INFORMATION

The first priority is to find what relevant information is available for a particular wildlife community or locality. Some things will never be found. Hardly any large scale maps were compiled in England before 1500, and it was not until the late 19th century that the area of every parish was accurately plotted and computed. In the search for what *is* available, the places to start are in the Local Studies Sections of the principal public libraries, and the County Record Office (Anon 1979). If they do not have what you want, they should know if and where it may be found. There are a number of published guides to historical sources, and many secondary works make use of these sources (Sheail 1980). The value of the university thesis should not be overlooked. A thesis, on a particular locality or region of interest, can be invaluable in identifying sources worth consulting. A select list of dissertations on British agrarian history has recently been produced (Morgan 1981). The search for relevant natural history records has been facilitated by the recent publication of a guide, which attempts to survey and list, for the first time, all the natural history manuscript resources preserved in the British Isles outside the Public Record Office (PRO) (Bridson *et al.* 1980).

It is paradoxical that those with the most intimate knowledge of the natural environment and its exploitation had the least need to record what they saw. For the landowner, tenant or labourer, there may have been some point in noting the presence of oaks, holly and other species of obvious economic or practical value, but the incidence of the wild service tree, orchids and the frog-bit pass unrecorded in estate papers and farm records. Many forms of management did not require anything to be written down, and accordingly no tangible record survives of their having occurred. To take one example, the practice of burning the heather on many uplands, often called muirburning, may be fundamental to an understanding of the course of change in plant communities, but few details of its incidence and frequency have been recorded for particular localities. A reference in a study of 'Wild England of to-day', published in 1895, describes how tracts of the Berkshire downlands were burned in March, leaving 'the good green undergrowth with invigorating ashes' (Cornish 1895). There was rarely any need to record such practices in estate records, and accordingly there are scarcely any detailed references to what could have been an important influence on the distribution of plant species in the downland turf.

It is not always necessary to go back to Romano-British times for the historical roots of the present day environment. As the famous French historian, Marc Bloch, remarked, "the explanation of the very recent in terms of the remotest past has ..... sometimes dominated our studies to the point of hypnosis" (Bloch 1954). In many instances, the most relevant historical events will date from the earlier years of this century. Fortunately, this is the period for which the evidence is most plentiful and varied.

Nevertheless, some reference must be made to the most famous historical source of all - the Domesday Survey of 1086, which identified the possessions of the principal landowners in the country. As well as information on taxes, human populations, ploughlands and plough teams, the Survey refers to woods, pastures, meadows, waste, saltpans and vineyards. It is an exceptional source in both an English and European context. As a medieval source of information, it is unsurpassed in its local, detailed information. The Domesday Survey does, however, highlight many of the problems inherent in historical documentation.

Like most historical records, the Survey is far from being a straight-forward document. The exact method of compilation and the precise meaning of many of the terms and measurements used remain obscure, and there are many inconsistencies in the presentation of data. It is impossible to be sure of the exact area and location of many woods and pastures mentioned in the Survey, and it is clear that some examples were omitted altogether. When Darby (1971) and his team of scholars tried to analyse and plot the data, all kinds of cartographic devices had to be used to surmount these difficulties. Darby concluded that what really emerged was an understanding of the geography of the Domesday Book. No one could be sure how closely this resembled the geography of Domesday England, but he believed there was good reason for thinking 'the broader features of the land utilisation of the time' had emerged. The remarkable thing about the Survey was not so much its 'tantalising obscurities', but the fact 'that King William's men did as well as they did' (Darby 1971). Similar comments might be made for almost every other source available to the historian.

THE PROBITY AND DETAIL OF THE EVIDENCE

Once a source has been identified, it is pertinent to ask what were the reasons for compiling and preserving the document, which is now being exploited for historical purposes. The answers obtained should decide how much reliance can be placed on the facts recorded. In view of the considerable use made of the maps and apportionments of the Tithe Commutation Survey in plotting the distribution of land use and ownership in the mid-19th century, it is salutary to learn that inaccuracies were consciously tolerated on the Tithe maps and in the apportionments, where these were in the general interests of administration (Evans 1978). Before using the large scale Ordnance Survey (OS) maps of the 19th century as a baseline for assessing changes in the length of watercourses, or the extent of woodland, rough grazing and water bodies, it is likewise relevant to discover more about the terms of reference given to both the field surveyor and draughtsman. In a geomorphological study of the drainage network within the New Forest perambulation, Ovenden (1981) concluded that the substantial changes revealed by a comparison of selected editions of the OS 1:10 560 and 1:2500 series maps reflected actual trends in networks, rather than differences in technique and presentation over the 50 year period. Detailed studies made by Harley (1979) have established that, until the first world war, the surveyors were expected to record land use and, until the mid-1880s, this information was actually published in the Parish Area Books.

The level of detail and accuracy sought from historical sources will vary according to the topic being studied. The Annual Returns, made by farmers to the Ministry of Agriculture, Fisheries & Food (MAFF) and its predecessor since the 1860s, identify the use of land and numbers and type of livestock kept on each holding. The ecologist will often find them inadequate, however, for his purpose. The parish is the smallest unit for which the statistics are available in the PRO. The parishes vary in size, and most contain a variety of farming conditions. Many farms transcend the parish boundaries (Coppock 1964).

The First Land Utilisation Survey was carried out in the 1930s on a national scale (Stamp 1962), and the second in the late 1950s. The published maps, where available, are usually too small in scale for the purposes of the ecologist, and reference should be made to the manuscript sheets, compiled in the field. These take the form of OS 1:10 560 sheets, on which land use was recorded, either by means of letters or colours, or a combination of both. The names of the surveyors, date of survey and of any revision, are given on the individual sheets; general details about land use or management may also be recorded in the margins. The maps of the First Land Utilisation Survey (where they survive) may be consulted in the British Library of Political and Economic Science, and those of the Second Survey in the Department of Geography, Kings College, London.

Far more abundant, and extending over a much longer time period, are the maps compiled for estate purposes, showing the outlines and subdivisions of an estate or farm-holding, and often a great deal of topographical information. An outstanding example is the 'Lanhydrock Atlas', compiled in 1693/94 at a scale of 1:4000, and covering 16 200 ha of a family's property in Cornwall. All the fields and garden plots are numbered, and a key gives their name, area and land use. Roads, water, arable, pasture, meadow, furze, commons, downland and cliff pasture, and areas wasted by mining, are distinguished. Pounds (1945) draws attention to how the in- and out-field system of land management can still be discerned in many of the manors. Even more plentiful are the leases, written surveys, correspondence and miscellanea that found their way into estate offices, safes and family boxes. In a study of the ecological history of the Lulworth-Tyneham area of Dorset, considerable help was derived from the unusually detailed covenants inserted into 18th century and 19th century leases, setting out the rotations and other husbandry practices to be followed by tenants. Landowners tried to prevent the over-exploitation of the heathland and valley bottoms as a source of fuel, and, in a lease for Tyneham Farm in 1848, the tenant was fined if the sward 'was destroyed or injured by stagnant water or by unnecessary poaching of livestock or other negligent or improper treatment' (Wells 1976).

Whether studying maps or a written text, it is important to interpret terms in the sense in which they were used at the time the documents were compiled. There is clearly the world of difference between the ecological impact of cultivation, land improvement and reclamation in the second half of the 20th century and that of the 19th century and earlier, and the use of such terms as 'arable', 'mown pasture', and 'drained lands' reflects this. It is also important to take account of the skills and prejudices of those compiling the documents. It has always been difficult to distinguish long leys from some forms of permanent pasture, or to define the boundaries between rough grassland, scrub and woodland. The fluctuating margins of waterbodies in wetland areas may also be described inaccurately. An even more difficult problem to resolve is that of deciding how far an historical source reflects the personal bias of the compiler. Many agricultural commentators set out to portray not so much the general pattern of farming but what should prevail if farmers were more progressive and successful.

The main interest of many ecologists will be in the changes that have taken place in the natural environment since the last war. The woodland ecologist is particularly fortunate because the census of woodlands, carried out by the Forestry Commission (FC) in the late 1940s, forms a remarkably detailed baseline from which to measure subsequent changes in the extent and character of woodlands. The published reports of this census have long been available and, since January 1980, it has been possible to consult the individual maps and records made for each individual woodland. The census drew heavily on the experience gained in partial surveys undertaken by the FC in 1938 and 1942. Samples of these surveys, together with the complete survey for the late 1940s, may be seen for England and Wales in the PRO, and those for Scotland in the Scottish Record Office.

Those seeking wartime baselines in the agricultural environment are less fortunate. The detailed information obtained by the National Farm Survey of the early 1940s will remain confidential to MAFF until the mid-1990s. The survey sought information not only on crops, livestock and the general facilities of each holding, but also on the conditions and standards of farming. In monitoring the changes that have taken place since the war, an obvious course might be to use the incidence of grant-aid as a guide to the pace and scale of land improvement. MAFF did not, however, make records of where grant-aid for ploughing up grassland or hedgerow removal was given. Fortunately, a set of master drainage maps was compiled between 1940 and 1980, indicating which fields were affected by grant-aided drainage schemes. MAFF is, however, precluded from allowing any information from these maps to be published, where this would allow drainage activities on individual holdings to be identified.

Perhaps the most useful evidence for the ecologist is a combination of documentary and field evidence in the form of old photographs, taken from the ground or air. It is not the purpose of this paper to describe in detail the availability and application of old air photographs in ecological studies but, where the location of the sites depicted in the photographs can be identified, they provide a unique type of baseline from which to measure subsequent changes. This has been graphically illustrated in a study of changes in Wistman's Wood on Dartmoor, where a comparison of ground photographs taken from the late 19th century onwards indicates the survival of many individual trees, a general rise in the canopy, change in tree-growth form, and expansion of the wood to nearly twice its former area (Proctor *et al.* 1980). The paper provides a valuable case study of the type of publications and repositories from which relevant photographs might be obtained. It is worth looking beyond local libraries, museums and record offices for material. It was *The Times* photographs library that provided the famous oblique air photograph published as the frontispiece to Tansley's *The British Isles and their vegetation,* showing the South Downs from a height of 6100 m in 1934 (Tansley 1939).

By collating the various pieces of historical information, it may be possible to indicate how long the plant communities on a site have been evolving, and thereby explain one of the causes for the variety of communities in a particular ecosystem. In a recent study of 12 selected areas of upland England and Wales, the maximum age of the present day moorland communities was postulated on the basis of information obtained from OS maps of different dates, and the incidence of plough marks within moorland areas shown on sorties of air photographs. Ball *et al.* (this symposium & 1981) and Parry *et al.* (1981) have recently completed this type of comparative study for the National Park areas of England and Wales, and have thereby indicated the striking loss of moorland core, particularly since the last war.

PAST, PRESENT AND FUTURE

To summarize, records of the annual state of vegetation and land use in Britain do not exist. Even if the resources for acquiring such knowledge have been available, it was never anyone's business to collect such data. Insights into the past are accordingly partial and spasmodic. Much has passed unrecorded. What is known cannot be submitted to trial and experimental proof. Before the ecologist decides to dismiss history as non-scientific bunk, he would do well, however, to recall how ecologists once thought the Norfolk Broads to be natural and how Tansley and other early ecologists mistook many of the downlands under cultivation in the 19th century to be sheepwalks since time immemorial. Not only will archive sources prevent the ecologist making blunders of this type, but knowledge of the past may provide a more precise understanding of what is happening today, and an invaluable perspective in forecasting how individual species, communities and the environment might develop in the future.

In this context, it is salutary to recall how the working papers of today will become the potential archives of tomorrow, providing an insight into the status of species or sites at specific points in time, and thereby establishing baselines for measuring the scale, rate and direction of change in the future.

We do not know precisely what questions the ecologist will be asking in 10, 30 or 50 years' time, but his dependence on such insights will be no less than it is today. Even the most pedestrian observations may be of some considerable future interest. Today, these records are stored not only in the form of the written word and conventional photography, but also in a machine readable form. Each constitutes a potential archive, and requires a conscious and systematic approach to its preservation.

REFERENCES

ANON 1979. *Record repositories in Great Britain.* London: HMSO for Royal Commission on Historical Manuscripts.

BALL, D.F., DALE, J., SHEAIL, J., DICKSON, K.E. & WILLIAMS, W.M. 1981. *Ecology of vegetation change in upland landscapes. Part I: General synthesis.* (Bangor occasional paper no. 2). Bangor: Institute of Terrestrial Ecology.

BLOCH, M. 1954. *The historian's craft,* 29. Manchester: Manchester University Press.

BRIDSON, G.D.R., PHILLIPS, V.C. & HARVEY, A.P. eds 1980. *Natural history manuscript resources in the British Isles.* London: Mansell.

CORNISH, C.J. 1895. *Wild England of to-day,* 174-175. London: Seeley.

COPPOCK, J.T. 1964. *An agricultural atlas of England and Wales.* London: Faber.

DARBY, H.C. ed. 1971. *The Domesday geography of eastern England,* p 2. Cambridge: Cambridge University Press.

EVANS, E.J. 1978. *Tithes and the Tithe Commutation Act 1836.* (Standing Conference for Local History). London: Bedford Square Press.

HARLEY, J.B. 1979. *The Ordnance Survey and land-use mapping: parish books of reference and the county series 1:2500 maps, 1855-1918.* (Historical geograph research series no. 2). Norwich: Geo Abstracts.

MORGAN, R. 1981. *Dissertations on British agrarian history.* Reading: Reading University and British Agricultural History Society.

OVENDEN, J.C. 1981. Hydrological data on large scale maps of the Ordnance Survey. *Cartogr. J.,* 18, 19-24.

PARRY, M., BRUCE, A. & HARKNESS, C. 1981. The plight of British moorland. *New Scient.,* 90, 550-551.

POUNDS, N.S.G. 1945. Lanhydrock atlas. *Antiquity,* 19, 20-26.

PROCTOR, M.C.F., SPOONER, G.M. & SPOONER, M.F. 1980. Changes in Wistman's Wood, Dartmoor: photographic and other evidence. *Rep. Trans. Devon. Ass. Advmt Sci.,* 112, 43-79.

ROWELL, T. 1981. Land use at Wicken Fen since *c.* 1600. *The history and management of Wicken Fen, discussion paper I,* 1-2. Cambridge: Cambridge University Department of Applied Biology.

SHEAIL, J. 1980. *Historical ecology: the documentary evidence.* Cambridge: Institute of Terrestrial Ecology.

STAMP, L.D. 1962. *The land of Britain, its use and misuse,* 20-41. 3rd ed. London: Longmans, Green.

TANSLEY, A.G. 1939. *The British Isles and their vegetation.* Cambridge: Cambridge University Press.

WELLS, T.C.E. 1976. *An ecological survey of the chalk and limestone grasslands on the Royal Armoured Corps Gunnery Ranges, Lulworth, Dorset,* 1, 52-54. (CST report nos. 47 & 48). Banbury: Nature Conservancy Council.

LAND CHARACTERISTIC DATA BANKS DEVELOPED FROM MAP-DERIVED MATERIAL

D F BALL, G L RADFORD AND W M WILLIAMS
Institute of Terrestrial Ecology, Bangor Research Station, Bangor

ABSTRACT

Ecological analysis and interpretation require the availability and accessibility of information about the physical environment. In Britain, such information is available nationally as maps or statistics but at a variety of scales and detail, and not in a convenient form for rapid quantitative and comparative reference. A common denominator between the map sources is the National Grid which provides recording cells appropriate to different levels of study. The grid cell approach to data extraction, storage, analysis and retrieval has been used in 2 projects at the Institute of Terrestrial Ecology, Bangor, which are dealt with in this paper. The first, a national land characteristic data set, covers Great Britain at the 10 x 10 km grid cell scale. The second used 0.5 x 0.5 km grid cells as the basis for land classification in a district study of upland land and its relationship to the distribution of moorland and grassland vegetation and to land use history.

INTRODUCTION

Ecological mapping could be defined in a limited sense as being concerned only with plant and animal species and communities. More correctly, it should also include land characteristics of the physical environment, because an understanding of ecosystems is impossible without environmental knowledge.

In many detailed ecosystem investigations, there is, of course, no substitute for the collation of new and existing land data specific to particular sites. No general-purpose data bank could provide all that is needed. Nevertheless, data banks of physical environmental information, with mapping facilities, can have important roles to play. They allow the initial selection of potential areas within which ecosystem studies should be located, and ensure comprehensive assessment of the possible options for such studies; they give, by direct correlation between recorded land characteristics and vegetation or fauna distribution, or by correlation of land classes and such distributions, a means of relating biological distributions to the physical environment; and they assist resource evaluation assessments at scales appropriate to the scale of the data set by giving statistical and map information on land character in a standard format. A natural resource information system is an 'integrated approach to collection, storage, manipulation, dissemination and use of resource data' (Mead 1981). Land characteristic data banks are a key element in such resource information systems.

There is an arguable case that the most desirable and effective support to ecological mapping that can be given by computer data-handling systems requires maximum accuracy in recording digitized data sets which, through map outputs, can allow retrieval of the exact locations of the input information. To supply such support requires sophisticated collection, storage and retrieval systems involving a major commitment of time, money and effort. However, it must be borne in mind that the original maps will always be available to return to when the exact locations of features are required, that features can change and hence maps become out of date, that some information sources are not of high precision, and that maps at any particular scale are selective in what they can include.

Our thinking with regard to land data sets for the Institute of Terrestrial Ecology (ITE), at this time, is that it is preferable to accept the use of less sophisticated methods, with less accurate but more rapid quantitative measurement of attributes from their source maps. Less sophisticated methods necessarily involve storage of data recorded for cells rather than for exact locations, the cells most conveniently being grid squares of the Ordnance Survey (OS) National Grid. This approach has allowed reasonably comprehensive land characteristic data sets for different purposes to be compiled relatively cheaply and quickly.

Two variants of the grid cell approach to land data collection and handling have been followed by ITE in recent years. The first (see Bunce *et al*. this symposium) uses a sampling procedure to record a wide range of attributes for a sample of grid squares. The second variant favours complete coverage, with data being recorded for all cells in the area of interest. Considered against the sampling approach, total coverage of all grid squares for any set of recorded attributes is obviously slower. However, what is recorded is factual for each square, within the limits of sources and the recording methods, rather than being probability assessments for a high proportion of them.

Pilot exercises at ITE Bangor used comprehensive data sets for a provisional land classification of the uplands of England and Wales at the 10 x 10 km scale, and for a district assessment in Snowdonia of land 'quality', in relation to agricultural and forestry potential, at the 0.5 x 0.5 km scale (ITE 1978). Subsequently, the 2 land data sets, which are discussed in this paper, have been produced. A land characteristic data bank for Great Britain has been assembled as a general-purpose source of information appropriate to national and regional scales of study. It is intended that this will remain valid and updatable over some years. At a larger scale, a land data set and a land classification based on this have been used in a study of vegetation and vegetation change in 12 upland areas.

NATIONAL LAND CHARACTERISTIC DATA SET

The National Land Characteristic and Classification (NLC) general-purpose data set at present stores 121 quantitatively determined attributes for each of the 2826 10 x 10 km grid squares recorded as containing land in Great Britain. The 7 land characteristic categories are summarized in Table 1. A full list of attributes, with details of their sources and methods of recording, will be included in a description of this data set it is planned to publish in 1982. They have been determined from maps of the most appropriate available scale, except for agricultural land use and population data which have been drawn from statistical sources.

Among the facilities offered by this data set are:

1. The presentation of standard statistical information on land characteristics for any 10 x 10 km grid square or combination of squares.

2. The identification, on maps and lists, of grid squares that meet a given specification. Because there is complete cover of the country, a search for grid squares with particular characteristics can be comprehensive rather than limited by personal knowledge. This may be particularly important for initial selection of areas justifying more detailed consideration as possible study locations.

3. The opportunity to relate recorded land characteristics, singly or in combination, to ecological distributions that have also been recorded at this scale.

4.   The ability, through direct display and tabulation, supplemented by classification analyses, to interpret the physical environmental range in Great Britain or its regions in ways that may prove helpful to illustrating or evaluating land resources in relation to ecology, economics and planning at national and regional scales.

TABLE 1   Attribute categories included for each grid square in the ITE
          10 x 10 km National Land Characteristic Data Set

Physiography:	Extent of land and sea
	Extent of altitude classes
	Altitude range
	Relative relief
	River frequency
	Extent of freshwater
	Length of coastline
Climate:	Extent of annual rainfall classes
	Short-term seasonal rainfall (from 3-year averages)
	Short-term seasonal air temperature
	Short-term seasonal sunshine
	Short-term seasonal windspeed
Geology:	Extent of stratigraphic units
	Extent of bedrock lithology categories
	Extent of surface geology categories
Soils:	Extent dominated by 8 major soil categories
Topography:	Settlement frequency
	Road frequency
	Railway frequency
	Total population
Land use:	Extent of farmland
	Extent of forest and woodland
	Extent of urban land
	Extent of individual agricultural crops
	Farm labour input
Agricultural land quality:	Extent in Agricultural Land Classification categories

As a small example of output statistics, Table 2 relates total values from the data set, drawn mainly from 1:250 000 OS or Ministry of Agriculture, Fisheries and Food (MAFF) maps, to other available measures of the same attributes. Total land areas recorded conform closely to official statistics, giving general confidence in the relatively rapid point-count method used for area assessment. Discrepancies between values for water body areas are attributable to the 1:250 000 source maps not showing small water bodies and not yet having included recent major reservoirs such as Kielder, Rutland and Brenig. The under-estimate of 'non-agricultural' land in the Agricultural Land Classification categories is because the MAFF area totals quoted (Agricultural Development and Advisory Service 1974) were taken from the original 1:63 360 maps produced, but the figures in the data set came from subsequently published 1:250 000 maps. In these, smaller areas of 'non-agricultural' land were, as a matter of policy, omitted and became part of the surrounding land of classes 1-5. In any land data set derived from maps, the nature and inevitable limitations of the source material must be clearly specified and understood.

TABLE 2   Areas for land use attributes (km^2) and human population, calculated from the National Land Characteristic (NLC) Data Set, and compared, as percentages, with equivalent values measured by other agencies

| | Great Britain | | England & Wales | | Scotland | | Comparable data – Reference |
	NLC Value	% equiv	NLC Value	% equiv	NLC Value	% equiv	
POPULATION	54 030 700	100.1	48 747 900	100.0	5 282 800	101.0	COI 1980
LAND:							
Total land	231 410	100.4	152 083	100.2	79 327	100.7	COI 1980
Freshwater	2 026	82.4	499	58.4	1 527	95.1	COI 1980
Agricultural Class 1	–	–	3 701	104.2	–	–	ADAS 1974
Class 2	–	–	19 122	107.1	–	–	ADAS 1974
Class 3	–	–	65 106	108.3	–	–	ADAS 1974
Class 4	–	–	26 429	108.6	–	–	ADAS 1974
Class 5	–	–	18 012	105.1	–	–	ADAS 1974
Non-agricultural	–	–	18 193	63.2	–	–	ADAS 1974
Farmland	170 557	95.7	114 640	98.5	55 917	90.3	Coppock 1974 & 1976
Barley	22 222	99.4	18 950	99.5	3 272	98.5	Coppock 1974 & 1976
Total crops	45 913	99.1	40 517	99.9	5 396	93.2	Coppock 1974 & 1976

NOTES:

NLC Data sources   - 'Land' and 'freshwater' from 1:250 000 OS maps; ALC categories from MAFF 1:250 000 maps (total land in England and Wales as measured from these in the ITE data set = 150 563 km^2, 99.0% of the land area as measured from OS maps).
- Population from Office of Population Censuses and Surveys statistics.
- 'Farmland' and 'crops' from statistics provided by the Edinburgh Computing Centre from MAFF and Department of Agriculture and Fisheries for Scotland data used by Coppock to prepare his Agricultural Atlases.

Figures 1-4 are examples of output maps from the line printer at ITE Bangor (more sophisticated output facilities are available on-line from other centres). They show a possible type of search pattern: identification of upland areas which might have unexploited forestry potential. An approach to such a search could use the following assumptions:

1.   that land between 244 and 427 m was particularly desirable (agriculture being assumed to have priority below 244 m, while land >427 m is assumed to be largely unsuitable for commercial forestry);

2.   that a significant extent of podzol soils would be advantageous (such soils, in moorland terms, can be thought of as at least relatively well-drained, they are found typically on moderate, and hence readily plantable, slopes, and, because they are generally unimproved, they are of relatively low financial value);

3.   that no significant forestry enterprise was already present.

At chosen levels of these specified characteristics, the altitude category (Figure 1) occurs in 16.5% of the total 10 x 10 km grid squares in Great Britain, while the soil category (Figure 2) occurs in 14.6% of them. Figure 3 shows that both specified characteristics are present in 6.1% of the squares (173 inland squares, occupying 17 300 km^2, or 7.5% of the land area of Great Britain). Of these 173 squares, 74 (Figure 4) presently have less than 10% forest. From such a search, accepting the assumptions made, upland areas of high potential for extensive forestry development, and hence of possible land use conflicts, have been located and found to occupy on a grid square basis 2.6% of Britain (the land in the squares being 3.2% of the land area of Britain). Further analysis within the main data set could explore other relevant factors for these squares, such as their present intensity of agricultural use assessed by stock density, or their climatic constraints assessed by average rainfalls and windspeeds. A supplementary data set will be able to identify possible administrative constraints, such as National Park or other designations. Surviving grid squares from such a reduction process could then be considered in more detail from source maps and in the field.

All the data that have been included in this 10 x 10 km land data bank already exist but it provides a co-ordinated, reasonably accurately quantitative information baseline that eliminates the need to search a range of sources on an *ad hoc* basis for each issue and study. The data set is intended to be open-ended and has a variety of uses. Particular applications may require additional data in existing or new categories which may either be retained as part of the main set, or discarded after their specific use. The permanent data can be upgraded by substituting more accurately measured attributes or by adding attributes from newly available sources.

There are, of course, inevitable constraints arising from the cell approach and the recording methods used. All that is possible from a grid cell output map is to know that some features (eg a particular altitude range, woodland, a soil class, a population level) co-exist within a grid square, not whether they coincide at a particular location. Such locations must be sought by following up the pointer provided by a grid cell search with a return to the source maps. Common combinations of factors cannot be so substantially reduced in their possible locations as can scarcer ones, but even in such uses it can be helpful to determine the possible geographic range over which these features occur. A second constraint is that grid square boundaries do not match administrative or natural geographic boundaries. Statistics and maps provided for administrative areas such as Counties or National Parks, or for geographic regions, must be

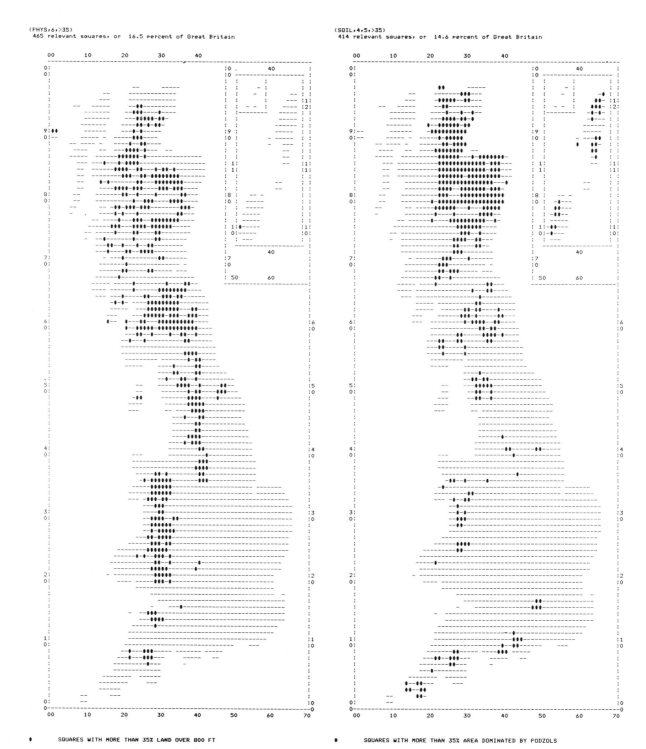

♦   SQUARES WITH MORE THAN 35% LAND OVER 800 FT

♦   SQUARES WITH MORE THAN 35% AREA DOMINATED BY PODZOLS

Figure 1   Line printer maps of grid squares meeeting an altitude specification

Figure 2   Squares meeting a soil specification

(PHYS,6,>35)AND(SOIL,4,5,>35)
173 relevant squares, or   6.1 percent of Great Britain

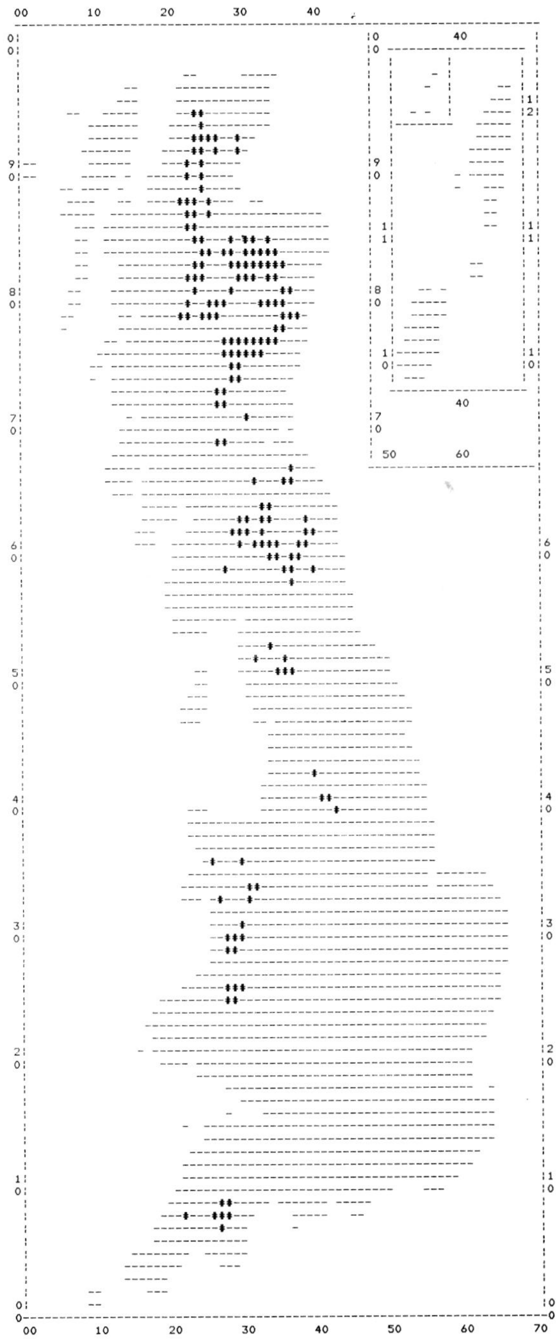

(PHYS,6,>35)AND(SOIL,4,5,>35)AND(USE,5,<10)
 74 relevant squares, or   2.6 percent of Great Britain

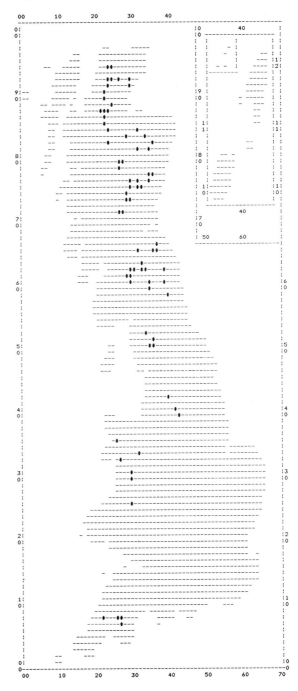

◆   SQUARES WITH MORE THAN 35% LAND OVER 800 FT, AND MORE THAN 35% DOMINATED BY PODZOLS

◆   SQUARES WITH MORE THAN 35% LAND OVER 800 FT, MORE THAN 35% DOMINATED BY PODZOLS,
AND WITH LESS THAN 10% WOODLAND COVER

Figure 3   Squares meeting both an
altitude and a soil
specification

Figure 4   Squares meeting altitude,
soil and forestry use
specifications

for the closest match of grid squares to the administrative or physiographic boundary. A third constraint is that information which can be retrieved and specifications which can be framed must be confined to the ranges recorded. For example, as the altitude ranges used in this data set include 0-61 m and 62-122 m (from contours transformed from feet), it is not possible to ask how much land below 100 m is in a square, or which squares have more than 80% of their area below 100 m. The data set cannot realistically cover all possible requirements, so these must be tailored to what is available.

UPLAND STUDY AREA DATA SET

The approach of measuring land characteristics of grid squares from existing map data and storing them in a computer in a form suitable for statistical and map outputs and for classification analyses has been applied at a district scale in a contract study, 'Ecology of Vegetation Change in Upland Landscapes', carried out by ITE for the Department of the Environment (Ball *et al.* 1981a, b). A data set, drawn mainly from 1:25 000 scale OS maps and covering 31 physiographic, topographic and rainfall attributes for 2977 0.5 x 0.5 km grid cells, has been used to analyse the land characteristics and permit a land classification of 12 parish areas spread through the uplands of England and Wales. The land analysis was part of an ecological study of grassland-moorland vegetation and its relationship to environment, recent land use history, and management.

The computer-stored, quantitative, land characteristic data set allows the retrieval of schematic grid cell maps to illustrate aspects of the environment of the study areas, and enables statistical comparisons to be made between areas. To give a simpler framework for discussion of contrasts and similarities between the scattered upland parishes and for interpretation of the environmental influence on vegetation distribution, a land classification was carried out using Indicator Species Analysis (ISA) (Hill *et al.* 1975) on a transformed set of land characteristics in a presence/absence form. ISA is a computer analytical method which successively divides a population of individuals to give 2, 4, 8, 16, etc, classes. It assesses the balance, in each individual, of a range of measured factors, in order to group together those individuals with the most similarity in selected significant properties (the 'Indicator Species' of the title, chosen in the analysis to give the clearest distribution between the 2 classes into which the whole or part of the population is divided at each stage of the analysis). The 'populations', in the cases referred to here, are a number of grid squares for which a series of land attributes are the measured factors, or they can be a series of plant records from sites, in which lists of plant species present are the measured factors, as in the original applications of the method.

Seven land types in 3 groups resulted from ISA, the average land character of which can be quantitatively defined in relation to the study areas as a group, by reference to the original map-derived data. The *'hill'* land group consists of 3 types, named as steep hill, hill and high plateau. All are dominated by altitudes above 427 m combined with low levels of settlement as shown by buildings, roads and field boundaries, but they are characterized by differences in their average relief and slopes. The *'upland'* land group, generally dominated by altitudes between 244 and 427 m, also contains 3 land types: steep upland, upland and upland plateau, again distinguished by their relief and slopes. All have relatively intensive settlement, particularly so in the upland land type. The seventh land type *'upland margin'* is dominated by low to moderate altitudes, moderate relief and low to moderate slopes, while having a relatively high settlement level. Within these classes determined by physiography and settlement pattern, rainfall phases can be separated at another level of classification.

Vegetation records were obtained from approximately 100 sites in grassland and moorland situations in the study areas, from which a vegetation classification provided 16 classes in 4 groups: improved pastures, rough pastures, grassy heaths and shrubby heaths. By treating the sites as a set of points which sampled grid squares classified in the 7 land types, the association between land type, as a simplification of a range of environmental factors, and vegetation class and group distribution has been used to interpret the present situation and to support predictions of possible changes in identified sectors of the study areas. These associations are discussed at length in the reports referred to (Ball *et al*. 1981a, b). Table 3 shows the broad association between vegetation groups at recorded sites and land types of the grid cells in which the sites fall. Grassy heaths are a particular feature of the landscape in steep upland and steep hill land types, while shrubby heaths are most prominent in the hill and high plateau land. Improved pastures play virtually no role in the hill land, while rough pastures, though not dominant in any land type, are particularly represented in upland margin, upland and steep upland land. Historical evidence of land use change between farmland and moorland over the past 200 years shows these 3 land types to have been the main focus of such change, 75% of all grid squares in which such change has occurred falling in 3 land types which occupy 41% of the total parish areas.

TABLE 3   The proportion (%) of different vegetation groups associated with 7 land types in 12 upland parishes, as recorded at *c*. 1000 sites

Land type	Vegetation group			
	Improved pastures	Rough pastures	Grassy heaths	Shrubby heaths
Steep hill		13	43	44
Hill		3	23	74
High plateau	2	5	21	72
Steep upland	19	23	42	16
Upland	44	25	9	22
Upland plateau	51	10	12	27
Upland margin	48	28	13	11

DEVELOPMENTS

Ecological mapping, as we have broadly defined it, involves both physical and biological data. At the 10 x 10 km scale, the biological component derives from the species distributions held at the Biological Records Centre (BRC), ITE Monks Wood. The availability of physical data for the same cell size as that of the BRC records provides an opportunity to re-address a number of questions left unanswered during early attempts to analyse the species distributions. The physical data set can be used to illustrate the existence, strength and geographical consistency of expected field correlations, for example between soil or geology categories and calcicole or calcifuge species. Further investigations can be made of less obviously related distributions with a view to identifying ecologically valid groupings of species at this broad scale. These groupings may be retained alongside the land characteristic data bank as associated material for subsequent retrieval and analyses.

A land characteristic data set on a grid cell basis at the 10 x 10 km scale has both a scientific value and a potential for application in strategic planning. Interest is consistently being expressed in the availability of data, and guidelines for their use, as aids to decision making in the planning process. The provision of 'ecological maps' of biological and environmental characteristics, and of land statistics, is an essential major component in resource assessment and development planning. Raster data, derived from gridded maps and satellite imagery, and vector data, derived from conventional maps or aerial photographs, are both likely to make contributions in this field.

Another intended development of the cell approach to mapping is to determine how classifications, to be derived from the National Land Characteristic and BRC data sets at the 10 x 10 km cell size, may be related to larger scales. The 0.5 x 0.5 km grid square data from upland areas could be extended to cover a sample of 10 km squares. It would then be possible to see whether 10 km squares, of a given national land class, consistently have a particular pattern of land types classified at the more detailed scale. There is also the opportunity to relate classes derived from the comprehensive 10 x 10 km land data set to those recognized in the 1 x 1 km data set of the Ecological Survey of Britain (see Bunce *et al.* this symposium).

From the alternative classification options which will be explored in this national data set, it is hoped that useful stable classes will result, giving the possibility of using stratified sampling to provide predicted values for additional ancillary attributes. This may be justified because predicted values are sufficient for the purposes in hand, or because data can only be obtained from a sample of squares. It must be borne in mind that sampling would not help in giving factual data for non-sampled cells, and that the sample population itself will not be appropriate for relating to other versions of a land classification.

In addition to the recorded quantitative data, and to grid square classifications that will simplify the range of land variation, and which will be stored as a second group of associated data, supplementary information likely to be used in conjunction with the main data set will be recorded for each 10 x 10 km cell. This third data group will provide an index to relevant scientific material, listing, for example, whether climatological stations, Forestry Commission census plots, National Nature Reserves, ITE or other Natural Environment Research Council study sites occur within a cell. This level of information will also include major conservation or landscape designations that place land use constraints on the square.

The view that a grid square approach to mapping simply displays statistics and cannot produce a 'real map' can be argued. However, grid square mapping has much to commend it as a means of presenting data in a readily appreciable form. The factual basis for conventional mapping at a level of accuracy appropriate to even medium scales for Britain does not yet exist over the full range of factors summarized in the national land characterization project. As such data become available they will increase the impetus to develop large digitized data bases, but the cell approach will retain a continuing, positive role in ecological investigation and mapping. At large scales the cell approach has a potentially direct link with remote sensing activities. Grid squares of 100 m or less, corresponding to squared pixel transformations of satellite data, may be used as sample units for ground truth, and as recording units for supplementary field survey data. The potential value of this combination in ecological survey and mapping has considerable appeal.

REFERENCES

AGRICULTURAL DEVELOPMENT AND ADVISORY SERVICE. 1974. *Agricultural land classification of England and Wales: presentation and exhibition*. Pinner: MAFF/ADAS Land Service.

BALL, D.F., DALE, J., SHEAIL, J., DICKSON, K.E. & WILLIAMS, W.M. 1981a. *Ecology of vegetation change in upland landscapes. Part I: General synthesis*. (Bangor occasional paper no. 2). Bangor: Institute of Terrestrial Ecology.

BALL, D.F., DALE, J., SHEAIL, J. & WILLIAMS, W.M. 1981b. *Ecology of vegetation change in upland landscapes. Part II: Study areas*. (Bangor occasional paper no. 3). Bangor: Institute of Terrestrial Ecology.

CENTRAL OFFICE OF INFORMATION. 1980. *Britain 1980: an official handbook*. London: HMSO.

COPPOCK, J.T. 1974. *An agricultural atlas of England and Wales*. London: Faber.

COPPOCK, J.T. 1976. *An agricultural atlas of Scotland*. Edinburgh: J. Donald.

HILL, M.O., BUNCE, R.G.H. & SHAW, M.W. 1975. Indicator species analysis, a divisive polythetic method of classification, and its application to a survey of native pinewoods in Scotland. *J. Ecol.*, 63, 597-613.

INSTITUTE OF TERRESTRIAL ECOLOGY. 1978. *Upland land use in England and Wales*. (CCP 111). Cheltenham: Countryside Commission.

MEAD, D.A. 1981. Statewise natural-resource information systems - A status report. *J. For.*, 79, 369-372.

A STRATIFICATION SYSTEM FOR ECOLOGICAL SAMPLING

R G H BUNCE, C J BARR AND HEATHER WHITTAKER

Institute of Terrestrial Ecology, Merlewood Research Station, Grange-over-Sands

ABSTRACT

Stratification procedures in ecology have not reached a comparable degree of sophistication to those in other biological disciplines, often relying upon intuition rather than a more systematic approach. Such a reliance upon personal judgement often leads to problems of consistency in interpretation and to the arbitrary selection of sample sites whose relationship to the whole area is insufficiently understood. The methods of stratification used in various branches of ecology are discussed, leading to the description of a system where personal judgement is reduced as far as possible. Strata are produced by objective analysis, from which a small number of randomly selected samples can then be drawn, known to be representative of the whole area. Because of this relationship, detailed studies carried out in these sample areas can be converted to overall estimates which can be subjected to tests of external validity and have statistical errors attached to them. The applications of this system to various types of ecological mapping are discussed.

INTRODUCTION

The advantages of stratified sampling in ensuring economy of expensive field studies have long been established. However, the majority of resource evaluation studies still largely rely upon complete coverage or non stratified random samples. Complete coverage leads to problems of sufficient consistency in recording and identification of precise categories. Stratified systems of sampling are more efficient in providing more accurate estimates with the same number of samples than random procedures and provide the main reason for the development of the system described below.

In contrast, the identification of social strata has proceeded to such an extent that many aspects of the human behaviour of the British people can be relatively accurately predicted from small samples. The measure of the success of such sampling may be seen by the efficiency of the advertising industry in the identification of consumer choices. The analysis of the natural environment is analogous to the sampling of human behaviour in that it involves simplifying multivariate data. In general, stratification is used for sampling in many disciplines but has not been widely applied in ecological science.

It is useful to summarize the approaches adopted by government agencies to various types of ecological surveys. First, the conservation bodies, whether of wildlife or landscape, rely principally upon individual recommendations for identification of key sites - as exemplified by the selective approach used by the Scottish Countryside Commission in setting up a series of scenic heritage areas in Scotland (Countryside Commission for Scotland 1978). Whilst such an approach may work well in finding unique sites, it is difficult to place these in the context of the country as a whole. Much commissioned research concerned with countryside, eg the monitoring of changes in landscape features, requires the identification of areas typical of the country as a whole, but often sites are selected arbitrarily for study, with no assessment of their degree of representation.

The annual reviews by the Ministry of Agriculture, Fisheries and Food (MAFF) and the Department of Agriculture and Fisheries for Scotland (DAFS) give total coverage but rely upon the accuracy of individual farmer's returns. Some stratification is used, however, when studies of different types of farm enterprises are undertaken. The various Forestry Commission censuses use different sampling patterns but do not employ external means of stratification. Similarly, maps of forest potential are based on complete coverage at low levels of detail. The Soil Survey, until recently, was concerned with detailed mapping at a local level, although this has been extended to both a larger scale for the whole country and at 10 km intersects. The Department of the Environment accumulates many types of data associated with ecological matters but invariably relies upon data submitted by component bodies with attendant problems of assessing relative accuracy. For example, as Coppock and Gebbett (1978) stated, there has been no co-ordinated survey of urban land, and the validity of the estimates that have been made is difficult to assess because of the variety of sources from which they were derived. The land utilization surveys of Stamp (1937-47) and Coleman (1961) rely upon complete coverage.

In vegetation science, sampling is usually by random or selective methods. Few attempts at external stratification have been made, with gradient analysis (Whittaker 1973) being comparable to the method described below, although not explicitly using stratification since vegetation and environment are treated as co-ordinates in a two-way diagram. Other ecological studies have used a comparable variety of regimes but examples of independent stratification have not been found. Finally, although technically extremely sophisticated, the analysis of various types of imagery generally attempts complete coverage - for example, there was little discussion of sampling presented in the papers concerned with remote sensing at this symposium.

The conclusion is that stratification is virtually unused. Moreover, the majority of national statistics do not have estimates of the errors attached to them and they have no external tests of validity. Advances in technology in the evaluation of resources have not therefore proceeded in parallel with advances in statistical procedures or data handling through computers.

THE LAND CLASSIFICATION SYSTEM

Many types of resource mapping attempt to derive homogeneous units, but in an ecological context these rarely exist. Heterogeneity is an integral feature of the natural world and any classification system should be designed to deal with it. Analogies may be drawn with taxonomy where many units can be readily recognized as distinct species but certain groups are difficult to differentiate. In the ecological field, difficulties are encountered for the same reason - continuous variation. Whilst the environment of Britain generally varies imperceptibly from one area to another, the objective of a land classification system is to produce classes that match the patterns that are present by helping to define boundaries. The more appropriate the analysis and data used, the better the classes will fit the natural patterns and the more efficiently they will be used as strata for sampling ecological parameters. The subjective observation of intercorrelations between ecological factors is the basis for the interpretation of ecological patterns in the field, and the land classification formalizes such intuitive ideas. The data necessarily consist of a large number of factors to adequately express the environment - single factors, such as altitude, are not useful on a national basis as they hold insufficient correlations - for example, an altitude of 300 m in Devon has different environmental implications from the same height in the north of Scotland.

The main objective of the system is to provide strata for ecological sampling in Britain. It is designed to reduce personal judgement to a minimum, although appropriate numerical methods need to be selected. The other 2 main objectives are to obtain a representative sample of the land use, vegetation and soils of Britain at a given time and to provide a basis for monitoring ecological change. Earlier studies are described by Bunce *et al.* (1975) and Bunce and Smith (1978).

The land classification has 3 phases:

1.   Land classification, based on environmental parameters.

2.   Ecological characterization.

3.   Prediction.

The first phase sets up classes corresponding to the 'x' axis of a regression, ie they act as independent variables. The classes are then used to make ecological observations, equivalent to the 'y' axes value of regression, ie the dependent variables. Intercorrelations between the 2 sets of factors can then be used to make predictions, the validity of which can be assessed according to independent, external criteria.

Land classification

The classes were determined by analysis of 282 attributes recorded from 1228 1 km squares, in a grid at 15 x 15 km intersections. Indicator Species Analysis (ISA) (Hill *et al.* 1975), a divisive, polythetic method of analysis, was used. This method divides the data hierarchically into classes that are relatively homogeneous, identifying indicator attributes at each stage. The data relate to climate, topography, geology and human artefacts recorded from maps. The analysis was used to define 32 classes. The indicator attributes alone can be used to assign any square in Britain to its appropriate class. In this way, the original 282 attributes were reduced to 76. A further 4800 squares have been assigned in this way, by using the key provided by ISA, in order to provide an estimate of the overall breakdown of each 1 km square in Britain to a land class. Increasing the sample number has been shown to modify only slightly the proportion of squares in each land class within a region, but does progressively increase the geographical resolution.

Ecological characterization

Eight squares were drawn at random from each of the 32 land classes. Vegetation data were recorded from 5 random quadrats in each square, with soil data being recorded from pits dug in the centre of each quadrat. Linear quadrats were also placed along hedgerows, running water and roadsides. The patterns of land use throughout the square were mapped, as well as other ecological information such as hedgerow length and woodland composition. The presence of other features, eg the breeds of livestock, was also recorded. The field procedure has subsequently been modified for differing objectives, eg for planning purposes, by the Highland Regional Council.

Prediction

The values from the squares are used to calculate the mean figures per land class for factors such as area of barley or hedgerow length. As the numbers of squares in Britain belonging to each land class are known, estimates can be obtained for any factor by summing the land classes for Britain as a whole. Descriptions of 2 land classes are given in Figures 1 and 2 to show the range of information that can be incorporated. Further estimates of land use potential or additional criteria can be assessed from the information contained in the series of sample squares. Predictive maps can also be made to indicate high concentrations of particular factors. Further information on the methodology is provided by Bunce *et al.* (1981a & b), and Benefield and Bunce (1982).

VALIDATION

Comparison with independent estimates

The figures published by MAFF and DAFS provide a convenient test of the sampling system and the estimates agree reasonably with them, particularly for crops with large areas. For example, the DAFS/MAFF figure for wheat (for 1977/78) was 1.16 x 10^6 ha, whereas the land classification figure was 1.11 x 10^6 ha, and for barley were 2.31 x 10^6 ha and 2.19 x 10^6 ha respectively. A complete table is given by Bunce *et al.* (1981a). Other published data show similar patterns of comparability with estimates from the land classification. The area of urban land estimated by Best (1976) was 20 517 km^2, whereas a preliminary estimate from the land classification was 22 242 km^2. Urban growth was estimated by Best (1976) at 148 km^2/year, whereas a trial study using the classification suggested that it continued at an average rate of 149 km^2/year between 1971 and 1981. A third example results from the MAFF study of improvable land carried out in 1980 in the north of England. Measurements were made of the area of Agricultural Land Classification (ALC) grades 4 and 5 for the entire region during the study and were subsequently repeated using a sample number of squares drawn from the land classification procedure. From the ALC map the proportions were 31.0% and 15.6% respectively, and from the land classification 26.1% and 15.7%.

Standard errors

Studies have commenced using the sample squares to calculate first the variances for the individual land classes and secondly those combined for Great Britain as a whole. Preliminary estimates show standard errors of the mean values to vary between 14.3% and 48.0%. Further work is needed on the distribution patterns within the data and on the efficiency of stratified as opposed to random samples. The effects of increasing the sample size as well as the theoretical background to the estimation of errors also need investigation.

Correlation

Various types of correlation analyses can be carried out to test the overall links between the environmental classification and the various sets of survey data. For example, the mean values of the reciprocal averaging ordination axes of the initial environmental data used to produce the land classification were calculated for each class. Component analysis was used to extract component values from the matrix provided by the mean values of the land use for each of the 32 land classes. Similarly, component values were extracted from the mean proportions of soil groups in the 32 classes. The correlation coefficients from the mean axis scores from the land classification were (both 30 df) 0.823 with the first component of the land use data and 0.923 with the first component of the soils data (P$\leq$0.001 in both cases). The procedure followed is comparable with that described by Fourt *et al.* (1971) and demonstrates the very high correlations present between the analysis of map data and subsequent field survey.

The conclusion to be drawn from the various validation exercises is that the 256 squares represent an adequate sample for many purposes, but that sample numbers from some classes need to be increased when examining particular parameters. The necessary sample number for a required accuracy can be calculated from the preliminary survey.

LAND CLASS SIX

TOPOGRAPHY

Mean max. altitude (m)	....	147
Mean min. altitude (m)	....	75
Altitude class	0- 76m.........	21
(mean	77- 198m.........	68
percentage	199- 488m.........	9
area)	489-1189m.........	-
Slope	(°)	4

CLIMATE

Mean min. temp. January	(°)..	2.8
Mean max. temp. July	(°)..	12.3
Mean soil deficit	(mm)..	6.0
Mean annual rainfall	(mm)..	11.1
Mean snowfall	(days)..	12.9
Duration bright sunshine	(hrs)..	6.2

SOILS

Mean pH	....	5.0
Mean loss on ignition (%)	....	15.3

Percentage of total area

Brown earths......................	45.0
Rendzinas.........................	5.0
Gleys.............................	22.5
Gleyed brown earths...............	10.0
Brown podsolic soils..............	-
Rankers...........................	2.5
Calcareous brown earths...........	-
Peaty podsols.....................	-
Podsols...........................	12.5
Peaty gleys.......................	2.5
Peats.............................	-

LAND USE

Percentage of total area

Wheat.............................	-
Barley............................	13.7
Other Crops.......................	2.9
Horticulture......................	0.2
Leys..............................	27.1
Permanent grass...................	30.0
Rough pasture.....................	-
Bracken...........................	0.3
Rushes............................	0.9
Moorland..........................	-
Peatland..........................	-
Mountain grass....................	1.3
Woodland..........................	10.8
Cliffs/sand/mud...................	-
Built-up..........................	11.6

NATIVE SPECIES

Percentage cover of major species

Perennial rye grass.....	20.0
Ling heather............	0.1
Common bent.............	6.5
Purple moor grass.......	-
Yorkshire fog...........	6.4
White clover............	3.0
Cocksfoot...............	4.0
Matgrass................	-
Bracken.................	1.5
Crested dogstail........	1.8
Italian rye grass.......	2.5
Timothy.................	3.1
Deer grass.............	-
Sheeps fescue..........	0.6
Creeping bent..........	3.4

LANDSCAPE

Barbed wire fences
Hedges managed
Hedges neglected
Hedges on banks
Hedgerow trees
Mature woodland
Gravel streams
Vernacular local
Slate roofs
Corrugated iron on roofs
Tracks
Farmhouse and farms

Figure 1   Description and occurrence of land class 6, gently rolling enclosed country; mainly fertile pastures

LAND CLASS TWENTY-TWO

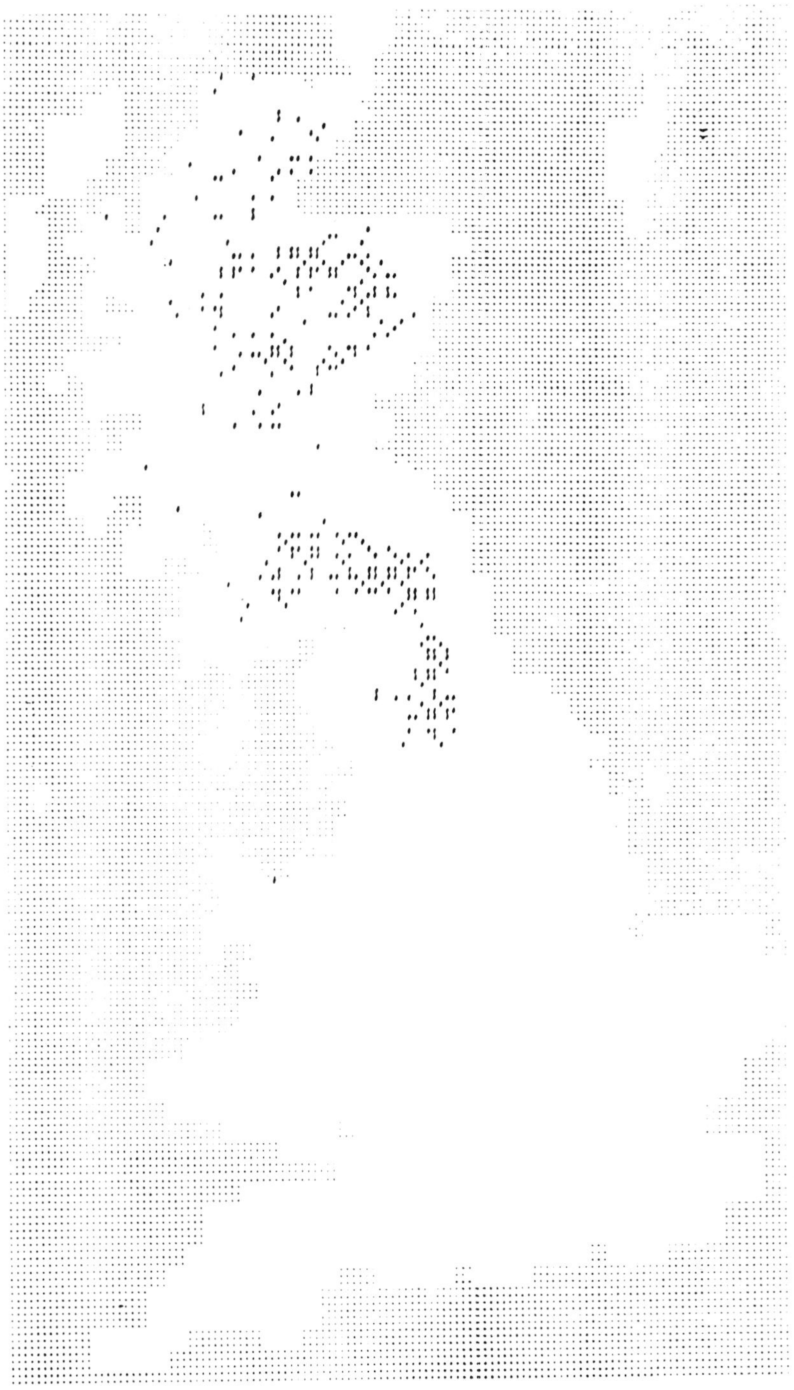

TOPOGRAPHY

Mean max. altitude (m)	....	430
Mean min. altitude (m)	....	298
Altitude class 0- 76m	....	-
(mean 77- 198m	....	2
percentage 199- 488m	....	87
area) 489-1189m	....	9
Slope (°)	....	8

CLIMATE

Mean min. temp. January	(°)..	-0.2
Mean max. temp. July	(°)..	19.0
Mean soil deficit	(mm)..	5.0
Mean annual rainfall	(mm)..	12.8
Mean snowfall	(days)..	51.6
Duration bright sunshine	(hrs)..	4.4

SOILS

Mean pH	4.5
Mean loss on ignition (%)	70.2

Percentage of total area

Brown earths.....................	10.0
Rendzinas........................	-
Gleys...........................	12.5
Gleyed brown earths..............	2.5
Brown podsolic soils.............	7.5
Rankers.........................	2.5
Calcareous brown earths..........	-
Peaty podsols...................	15.0
Podsols.........................	-
Peaty gleys.....................	32.5
Peats...........................	15.0

LAND USE

Percentage of total area

Wheat.........................	-
Barley........................	2.1
Other Crops...................	1.4
Horticulture..................	-
Leys..........................	0.9
Permanent grass...............	6.5
Rough pasture.................	1.6
Bracken.......................	1.1
Rushes........................	3.3
Moorland......................	25.6
Peatland......................	12.1
Mountain grass................	-
Woodland......................	34.9
Cliffs/sand/mud...............	1.1
Built-up......................	1.6

NATIVE SPECIES

Percentage cover of major species

Perennial rye grass.....	2.8
Ling heather............	28.9
Common bent.............	0.3
Purple moor grass.......	3.9
Yorkshire fog...........	0.8
White clover............	3.3
Cocksfoot...............	0.1
Matgrass................	0.3
Bracken.................	1.8
Crested dogstail........	0.5
Italian rye grass.......	-
Timothy.................	0.3
Deer grass.............	0.3
Sheeps fescue...........	1.1
Creeping bent...........	-

LANDSCAPE

Woodlands over 5 ha.
Stones/rocks
Lines of shrubs

Figure 2   Description and occurrence of land class 22, margins of high mountains, moorlands, often afforested

APPLICATIONS

Many of the potential applications of the system are demonstrated by the project currently being undertaken under a contract with the Department of Energy (Bunce *et al.* 1981c). The main objective of this study is to estimate the area of land in Britain that could be available for wood energy plantations under various constraints, both financial and institutional. A representative series of squares was submitted to other programme participants (cf MacDonald *et al.* 1981) who assessed the net present values of the current agricultural pattern and the potential of conventional forestry, of single stem trees for energy, and of coppice trees for energy. The probability of institutional constraints upon forestry development was defined by examining their occurrence on the base maps. Each square therefore had a series of overlays for which the overlaps were successively calculated to determine which land use or potential land use would have the highest yield in economic terms. The institutional constraints were then superimposed at successive probability levels to examine their effect. Various discount rates and different markets, eg methanol or synthetic natural gas, were then taken in order to investigate the sensitivity of the availability of land to economic factors. Each land class is treated separately, the individual estimates being combined to obtain figures for Britain as a whole. Land classes with high potential can then be defined, regional predictions made and the principal patterns of likely availability described for the whole of Britain.

This project shows how the system can be used to obtain estimates of potential for Britain from a small number of sample squares. The framework of the land classes is being used to assess the sensitivity of the land use patterns in Britain to changes in basic economic assumptions. Pilot studies were used for representative classes to focus the study on areas identified as being of significance so that expensive trials are avoided. It is of particular importance that the estimates are related back to identifiable areas of land rather than synthetic units. These areas can be identified subsequently for experimental field studies.

The principle of applying various constraints to the potential of land in a representative series of samples is widely applicable in environmental impact studies. The effect of various potential changes can be compared overall and those likely to affect the system to a major degree could be identified. In a different type of study, the strata are being used to identify populations for genetic studies. The validity of small numbers of samples allows regular monitoring and the potential of the land classification for following habitat or landscape change is therefore under consideration. It is planned to monitor the loss of agricultural land to urban development in a similar way, with increases in sample number for some classes being incorporated in order to attain the required accuracy. At a regional scale, studies are in progress to set up a local series of representative squares for sampling rural land use, but which at the same time co-ordinate with the national series of land classes. A comparable local study has derived land classes to provide an unbiased stratification for assessing pollution levels and monitoring changes. In all such studies, the potential for change can be examined efficiently by reducing the requirement for field studies and identifying the topics likely to be profitable for future work.

CONCLUSION

Stratification is rarely used in ecological surveys. The system described uses defined environmental strata that have been shown to be relevant to the survey of a range of ecological factors. The data from strata can be subjected to tests of statistical accuracy and external validity. They provide a framework for measuring current and potential land use and enable the sensitivity of the proportions of the land surface of Britain to various changes to be assessed.

REFERENCES

BENEFIELD, C.B. & BUNCE, R.G.H. 1982. *A preliminary visual presentation of land classes in Britain.*   (Merlewood research and development paper no. 91). Grange-over-Sands: Institute of Terrestrial Ecology.

BEST, R.H. 1976. The extent and growth of urban land. *The Planner,* 62, 8-11.

BUNCE, R.G.H., MORREL, S.K. & STEL, H.E. 1975. The application of multivariate analysis to regional survey. *J. environ. Manage.,* 3, 151-165.

BUNCE, R.G.H. & SMITH, R.S. 1978. *An ecological survey of Cumbria.* Kendal: Cumbria C.C. and Lake District Special Planning Board.

BUNCE, R.G.H., BARR, C.J. & WHITTAKER, H.A. 1981a. An integrated sysem of land classification. *Annu. Rep. Inst. terr. Ecol. 1980,* 28-33.

BUNCE, R.G.H., BARR, C.J. & WHITTAKER, H.A. 1981b. *Land classes in Great Britain: preliminary descriptions for users of the Merlewood method of land classification.* (Merlewood research and development paper no. 86). Grange-over-Sands: Institute of Terrestrial Ecology.

BUNCE, R.G.H., PEARCE, L.H. & MITCHELL, C.P. 1981c. The allocation of land for energy crops in Britain. In: *Energy from biomass,* edited by W. Palz, P. Chartier and D.O. Hall, 103-109. London: Applied Science.

COLEMAN, A. 1961. The second land use survey: progress and prospect. *Geogrl J.,* 127, 168-186.

COPPOCK, J.T. & GEBBETT, L.F. 1978. *Land use and town and country planning.* (Reviews of U.K. statistical sources 8). London: Pergamon.

COUNTRYSIDE COMMISSION FOR SCOTLAND. 1978. *Scotland's scenic heritage.* Perth: C.C.S.

FOURT, D.F., DONALD, D.G.M., JEFFERS, J.N.R. & BINNS, M.O. 1971. Corsican pine (*Pinus nigra* var *maritima* (Ait.) Melville) in southern Britain: a study of growth and site factors. *Forestry,* 44, 189-207.

HILL, M.O., BUNCE, R.G.H. & SHAW, M.W. 1975. Indicator species analysis, a divisive polythetic method of classification and its application to a survey of native pinewoods in Scotland. *J. Ecol.,* 63, 597-613.

MacDONALD, D.W., BUNCE, R.G.H. & BACON, P.J. 1981. Fox populations, habitat characterization and rabies control. *J. Biogeogr.,* 8, 145-151.

STAMP, L.D. 1937-1947. *The land of Britain: The final report of the Land Utilisation Survey of Britain.* In 92 parts of 9 volumes. London: Geographical Publications.

WHITTAKER, R.H. 1973. *Ordination and classification of communities.* The Hague: Junk.

IV TECHNIQUES OF SURVEY

THE BRITISH RAIL LAND SURVEY

CAROLINE SARGENT
Institute of Terrestrial Ecology, Monks Wood Experimental Station, Huntingdon

ABSTRACT

A multivariate geographic classification was prepared and used to structure an ecological survey of British Rail land. Existing land classifications refer to cellular units and could not be adapted to this study because there is no constant relationship between the length of railway line crossing a cell and the area of land within that cell.

INTRODUCTION

The British Rail (BR) Land Survey has developed in response to concern about structural and qualitative changes in railway vegetation. These result from a radical post-war reduction and alteration in verge and cess (track bed) management practices. The purpose of the Survey is to provide baseline information by recording, classifying and mapping the distribution of vegetation types and species. The information will be used to measure further change and is fundamental to management and conservation decisions.

There are 18 200 km (11 300 miles) of operational BR line throughout Britain. A safety constraint limited the work to rural verges which cover 30 678 ± 1 121 ha. The Survey was structured to combine objective sampling, which would provide the information to classify and map the distribution of vegetation, with visits to sites of suspected biological interest. These latter were intended to ensure that a large proportion of areas of potential conservation value were described.

Originally the Survey was based on random sampling (Way *et al*. 1978). At that time,it was recognized that the distribution and representativeness of sampling could be improved by stratification (Lakhani this symposium), although information (such as soil pH or the slope or aspect of the verges) likely to reflect the distribution of vegetation was either not available or existed only at impractical scales. However, an alternative approach has been to use a multivariate classification of mapped (available) geographic attributes to structure a survey. Derived classes are used as strata, and samples are proportionately distributed between, and randomly selected within, these classes (Bunce *et al*. 1975). Land classifications at different scales and based on different assumptions are available for stratifying ecological survey (Bunce *et al*. and Ball *et al*. this symposium), but in all cases refer to cellular units of land. They could not be applied to the BR Survey as there is no constant relationship between the length of line crossing a cell and the area of land within that cell.

Because of this linear constraint, a new geographic classification, relating strictly to rural railway land, was made. This paper describes the BR classification and its application to survey, and discusses the value of the stratification method in terms of some field-collected data.

TABLE 1 Constant attributes of the 26 railway track classes distinguished by classification of 83 geographic attributes using Indicator Species Analysis. Only attributes occurring in at least 80% of track class members (10 mile units) are shown. The Table is ordered with an index derived from the first axis of a Reciprocal Average Ordination

Attribute	Southern Chalk Uplands	South Eastern	Chilters	South Coastal	Weald	South Midlands	Midlands & East Anglia	Northern Sandstones	Fens	Eastern Lowlands	Central Southern	South Western	West Coastal	Lancashire Plain	Pennine Coal Measures	Scottish Lowlands	Midland Hills	Pennines	Western Coal Measures	North West Coastal	North Coast Carboniferous	Welsh Uplands	Igneous Coastal	Central Highlands	Highland Coastal	West Highlands
<7.0C January	x	x			x																					
Well drained calc. soils	x							x																		
>6.0 hrs sun July	x	x	x	x	x					x		x	x													
Chalk and oolites	x										x															
<10 days snow cover		x		x									x	x	x	x										
Electrified		x	x														x									
<400' ASL	x					x	x									x				x						
<25' ASL				x					x																	
Alluvium		x				x							x													
Drift			x	x	x					x	x	x	x					x	x			x				
Stagnogleys						x	x	x							x	x					x					
<6.0 hrs sun July						x				x		x	x					x								
<20 days snow cover						x	x	x	x	x					x	x					x			x		
<100' ASL									x		x	x	x	x	x			x								
Salt marsh									x																	
Bunter															x	x										
Coal measures															x				x	x	x					
<200' ASL											x				x	x					x				x	
<30 days snow cover																	x									
<6.0C January										x	x				x								x			
Non-calc. brown earths												x	x	x		x			x		x					
<5.5 hrs sun July													x	x	x	x					x					
<6.5C January															x	x										
Carboniferous & magnesian															x						x					
Igneous & intrusive																					x					
<400' ASL															x									x		
Boulder clay																			x	x	x			x	x	x
Lowland podzols																								x	x	
Heath/rough pasture																			x	x				x	x	x
Single track																							x	x	x	x
Metamorphic																										x
Upland gleys																										x

TRACK CLASSIFICATION AND SAMPLING

The rural railway network was divided into 899 measured 10 mile (16.1 km) units, coincident with BR ¼ mile posts. Selected mapped attributes were scored, where they abutted on to, or were crossed by the railway line, for each of these units (Sargent & Mountford 1980). The information was classified using Indicator Species Analysis (Ball *et al.* this symposium; Hill *et al.* 1975), a polythetic divisive method based on correspondence analysis. After inspection and some modification, the classification yielded 26 track classes (ie groups of 10 mile units). Constant attributes, which are present in more than 80% of members of each track class, are shown in Table 1. The Table is ordered using an index derived from the relative representativeness of each attribute within each track class, and is designed to show relationship between classes. There is an evident gradient between lowland south eastern and upland north western classes. Some classes are more heterogeneous than others: for example, there are only 2 constant attributes in the large (70 units) class 'Midlands and East Anglia', whereas 'Pennine Coal Measures' (51 units) has 7 constant attributes, and the smaller class 'Weald' (28 units) has 6. The average number of 10 mile units per class is 36, and the mean number of attributes, 5.

A total of 480 sites was distributed proportionately between track classes. Units to be sampled were randomly selected, and 100 m sampling sites located at randomly chosen BR mile posts within the track class unit. For practical purposes, sites were restricted to areas of convenient access. Four transects were measured at each site at right angles to the track, the direction which, within a short stretch of line, usually includes most variation. A number of 2 x 2 m quadrats, strictly proportional to the width of the verge, were distributed along each transect. Species cover and height were recorded, and pH and certain other environmental measurements taken. Species lists for entire sites were made.

The track classification has been digitized and mapped by the Natural Environment Research Council's Experimental Cartography Unit, and, as an example, the distribution of track classes and sample sites in the London Midland Region is shown in Plate 1.

VEGETATION CLASSIFICATION

A synopsis of a working classification of railway grasslands and tall herb communities showing constant species (present in >80% of like samples) is given in Table 2. The minimum cover value recorded for each constant species in at least 75% of samples is also given. The cover values are from the following simplified scale:

<1	1
1-10	2
11-25	3
26-50	4
51-100	5

The classification is of information from a subset of 120 sites (937 samples) distributed proportionately within the 26 track classes. The classification method used was TWINSPAN (Hill 1979), a FORTRAN program based on correspondence analysis, which produces an ordered two way table by the grouping of both samples and species. After inspection, some modifications were made and the vegetation divided into 24 working classes, which will be tested against the entire data set. Scrub and secondary woodland classes have, for simplicity,

TABLE 2   Synopsis of a working classification by TWINSPAN of 937 railway grasslands and tall herb communities

	Upland bent/fescue	Grass heath	Bent/fescue	Coarse fescue	Neutral fescue	Ruderal/fescue	Calcicolous grassland	Heath false brome	Species rich false oat	Coarse false oat	False oat and bramble	Creeping soft grass	Meadowsweet	Nettle/false oat	Tall herb and bramble
No of samples	7	17	14	62	43	18	9	17	37	114	115	18	19	58	90
Agrostis tenuis	5	3	4												
Festuca rubra	2	1	4	3	4	3	3	2	2	2					
Galium saxatile	2														
Juncus effusus	2														
Arrhenatherum elatius				2	2			2	4	4	4	2	1	4	
Holcus lanatus				1											
Plantago lanceolata					1	2	1								
Dactylis glomerata				1	1			1		2					
Fragaria vesca							2								
Chrysanthemum leucanthemum							2								
Brachypodium pinnatum									5						
Rubus fruticosus											2				1
Holcus mollis												3			
Filipendula ulmaria													4		
Urtica dioica														2	4
Galium aparine														1	1

been pooled (their identification is not central to the discussion) and grasslands and tall herb communities occurring in fewer than 7 samples have been excluded from the synoptic table. Thus, for example, *Molinia* grasslands (close to the *Molinia-Myrica nodum* of McVean and Ratcliffe 1962) which were largely restricted to the West Highland line (Sargent & Mountford 1981) and common reed (*Phragmites australis)* beds, which occur on some embankment footings, are not included.

For convenience, in this paper, the working vegetation types have been given brief English names. Detailed phytosociological information will be published elsewhere.

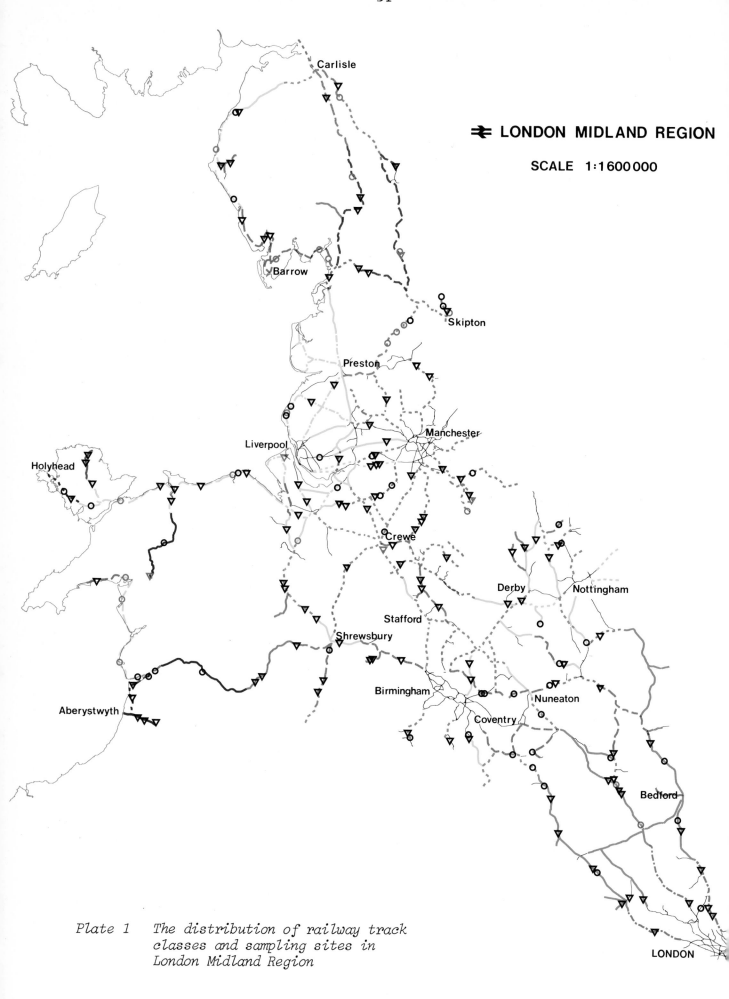

⇌ **LONDON MIDLAND REGION**

SCALE 1:1600000

Carlisle

Barrow

Skipton

Preston

Holyhead

Liverpool

Manchester

Crewe

Derby

Nottingham

Stafford

Shrewsbury

Birmingham

Nuneaton

Coventry

Aberystwyth

Bedford

LONDON

*Plate 1   The distribution of railway track
classes and sampling sites in
London Midland Region*

LEGEND

TRACK CLASSIFICATION

—————————	South Eastern
··················	Weald
— — — — — —	Southern Chalk Uplands
—·—·—·—·—·—	Chilterns
—————————	South Western
·················	Central Southern
— — — — — —	South Coastal
—————————	South Midlands
·················	Midlands and East Anglia
— — — — — —	Eastern Lowlands
—·—·—·—·—·—	Fens
—————————	Pennine Coal Measures
·················	Northern Sandstones
— — — — — —	West Coastal
—·—·—·—·—·—	Lancashire Plain
·················	Pennines
—————————	Western Coal Measures
— — — — — —	Midland Hills
—————————	North Coast Carboniferous
·················	Scottish Lowlands
— — — — — —	North West Coastal
—————————	Highland Coastal
·················	West Highlands
— — — — — —	Central Highlands
—————————	Welsh Uplands
·················	Igneous Coastal

SAMPLING SITES

▽	Random
○	Biological Interest
◻	Cutting / Embankment
▼	Random - revisited during 1981

SITES OF PARTICULAR BIOLOGICAL INTEREST

▽	Random
○	Biological Interest
◻	Cutting / Embankment
▼	Random - revisited during 1981

Cartography by the Experimental Cartography Unit

THE DISTRIBUTION OF VEGETATION TYPES

Broadly, the classification distinguishes between vegetation which is dependent on the disturbed railway environment, and that which occurs, although comparatively uninfluenced, where the take of railway land is sufficiently great.

TABLE 3   Distribution of vegetation types within track classes

	Scottish Lowlands	South Western	Midlands & East Anglia	West Coastal	South Midlands	Pennines	Pennine Coal Measures	Southern Chalk Upland	Midland Hills	Northern Sandstones	Weald	North Coast Carboniferous	Chilterns	Central Southern	Central Highlands	Western Coal Measures	Eastern Lowlands	South Eastern	West Highlands	Igneous Coastal	Fens	Highland Coastal	Lancashire Plain	Welsh Uplands	South Coastal	North West Coastal	TOTAL
Tall herb and bramble	x		x	x	x	x	x	x	x	x	x	x	x	x	x		x	x	x	x	x		x	x	x	x	23
Coarse false oat	x	x	x	x	x	x	x		x	x	x	x	x	x	x	x	x			x	x	x	x	x		x	22
False oat and bramble	x	x	x	x	x	x	x	x	x	x	x	x	x		x	x	x	x		x	x		x				20
Coarse fescue	x	x	x	x	x	x	x		x	x	x				x	x	x			x			x		x	x	17
Nettle/false oat	x		x	x	x	x	x	x	x		x				x	x	x				x	x	x		x		16
Species rich false oat	x		x	x	x	x	x	x			x		x	x	x				x					x			13
Neutral fescue	x	x	x			x	x	x		x		x			x	x				x							11
Ruderal/fescue		x		x	x	x	x	x			x				x					x							9
Grass heath	x		x	x		x	x					x			x				x								8
Meadowsweet		x		x							x	x	x	x			x										7
Creeping soft grass	x		x	x		x					x				x	x											7
Bent/fescue	x					x	x				x	x							x					x			7
Heath false brome																			x			x					2
Calcicolous grassland								x																			1
Bramble, scrub and secondary woodland	4	9	3	6	4	2	1	4	5	3	3	2	4	3	1	3	1	3	4	1	1	3	1	2	4	2	79
No. types/class	14	14	13	13	12	12	12	11	11	11	10	10	9	9	9	9	7	7	7	7	6	6	6	6	6	5	242

Table 3 shows the distribution of vegetation types within track classes. The Table is ordered so that the most widespread vegetation (ie occurring in most track classes) and track class (ie including the largest numbers of vegetation types) are given respectively in the first row and column. There is no correlation between all track and vegetation classes, and there is no strong correlation (r = 0.565) between the verge area of each track class and the number of vegetation types present (Figure 1). However, a clear pattern exists within Table 3: vegetation associated with disturbance is widespread, whilst vegetation independent of railway influence has a more restricted distribution. Coarse false oat grassland occurs in 22 of the 26 track classes. The grassland shows a preference for embankment slopes where ballast has been tipped, but is generally abundant on ungrazed verges. False oat is not present in the 2 North West Scottish classes, where soil and climate conditions are extreme. It is also absent from the 'Southern Chalk Uplands', where herb rich fescue grasslands are predominant, and from 'South Eastern', where very little present management has been recorded and bramble has become ubiquitous. Absence from the latter 2 classes may be an artefact of the smallness of the subset of samples.

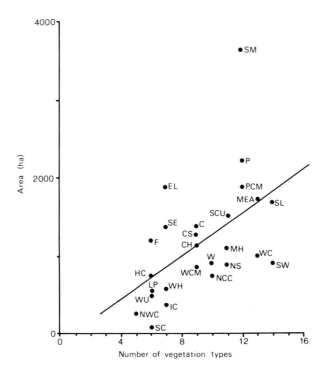

Figure 1   The number of vegetation types per track class against track class area is shown. All vegetation types, including scrub and secondary woodland, are given.   Track class names are abbreviated to initials:

SCU Southern Chalk Uplands   SE South Eastern   C Chilterns   SC South Coastal W Weald   SM South Midlands   MEA Midlands & East Anglia   NS Northern Sandstones F Fens   EL Eastern Lowlands   CS Central Southern   SW South Western   WC West Coastal   LP Lancashire Plain   PCM Pennine Coal Measures   SL Scottish Lowlands MH Midland Hills   P Pennines   WCM West Coastal Measures   NWC North West Coastal NCC North Coast Carboniferous   WU Welsh Uplands   IC Igneous Coastal   CH Central Highlands   HC Highland Coastal   WH West Highlands

Bent/fescue grassland, on the other hand, is found in only 7 of the track classes; these all occur in upland north and west Britain. Heath false brome grassland,on railway verges,is virtually restricted to calcareous cuttings in Eastern Region, and the herb rich fescue grassland, called here, loosely, 'Calcicolous', is recorded only from unstable chalk slopes in the class 'Southern Chalk Uplands'.

Ideally, a stratification of railway land would accommodate such widely differing distributions. However, there are several factors which deflect the establishment and development of vegetation which might otherwise be expected to occur locally. In particular, edge effects along this linear environment are important. These arise both from track maintenance and from adjacent land usage.

Vegetation within 3-4 m of the track and growing on embankment slopes tends to be disturbed by chemical spraying, cutting, waste disposal from trains and the cyclical dumping of spent, often oily, ballast. Along main lines, ballast is replaced about every 5 years. False oat grass, which is known as a

primary colonizer of limestone screes in Derbyshire (Pfitzenmeyer 1962), tends
to spread rapidly on to spent ballast, which also provides a habitat for such
characteristic railway plants as Oxford ragwort (*Senecio squalidus*), small
toadflax (*Chaenorhinum minus*) and spear leaved willow herb (*Epilobium lanceo-
latum*) which is now found to be increasing its range. Particularly where there
is nearby woodland, bramble spreads on to such tips, whilst some ephemerals and
annuals, including lamb's lettuce (*Valerianella locusta*) and stinking groundsel
(*Senecio viscosus*), grow where the spent material is fine grained or cindery.
Other plants, such as the common horsetail (*Equisetum arvense*) and the bonfire
site moss (*Funaria hygrometrica*) show resistance to the chemical sprays in use,
or, as spring whitlow grass (*Erophila verna*), avoid disturbance by completing
their life cycles before spraying occurs in early summer. This kind of influence
from track maintenance is ubiquitous along cess margins, and produces a vegetation which is similar throughout BR land.

Effects from adjacent land usage are clearly more diverse, and include such
variables as agricultural spray drift, the grazing of a marginal strip in
pastoral land, dumping of garden rubbish and propagules, and seeding and shading
from coniferous plantations. Where these edge effects (cess and boundary) are
small compared with the width of the railway verge, the vegetation is usually
modified by previous management practices. Since 1960, however, only sporadic
or *ad hoc* clearance of the verges has occurred. Whilst the general approach to
maintenance, prior to this date, is well known - verges were scythed and burnt
once or twice annually, and most invasive scrub cut and cleared - there are no
areas for which a documented and continuous record of the work done exists.

A very important influence on the distribution of vegetation is the slope
angle and kind (embankment, cutting, flat) of formation. Slope and angle clearly
affect drainage, insolation and exposure, whilst the kind of formation may
determine the quality of the soil. Embankments were built from available
materials, and often topsoiled, whilst cuttings were merely excavated. Fine
leaved and species rich grasslands, and scrub and secondary woodland, characteristic of local soil or climatic conditions, are usually found on cutting slopes.
These tend to have a low soil nutrient status and are comparatively uninfluenced
by track management. The fine leaved grasslands were maintained by cutting and
burning, and it is probable that many are now being replaced by woody species.
This kind of information was not available prior to field sampling, and it is
clear that the man-made and disturbed linear railway environment is, to some
extent, independent of the local soil and climatic conditions reflected in the
stratification. This independence is confirmed by the lack of correlation
between vegetation and track classes (Table 3), despite the distribution pref-
erences shown by some vegetation types. The stratification can be amplified
with field-collected data, although its predictive value remains limited because
there is so much, and such variable, disturbance.

Nevertheless, use of multivariate classes to stratify the system has
ensured a good distribution of samples, and has given rise to smaller and comparatively homogeneous units, amenable to analysis, interpretation and discussion. It has also provided a framework for looking at the potential value of BR
land in terms of management for conservation purposes.

ACKNOWLEDGEMENTS

This work was carried out under contract with the Nature Conservancy
Council. I am most grateful to Mr J O Mountford for help with data collection
and to Dr R G H Bunce for providing stimulus to the work.

REFERENCES

BUNCE, R.G.H., MORRELL, S.K. & STEL, H.E. 1975. The application of multivariate analysis to regional survey. *J. environ. Manage.*, $\underline{3}$, 151-165.

HILL, M.O. 1979. *TWINSPAN: a FORTRAN program for arranging multivariate data in an ordered two way table by classification of the individuals and attributes*. Ithaca, New York: Cornell University.

HILL, M.O., BUNCE, R.G.H. & SHAW, M.W. 1975. Indicator species analysis, a polythetic method of classification, and its application to a survey of native pinewoods in Scotland. *J. Ecol.*, $\underline{63}$, 597-613.

McVEAN, D.N. & RATCLIFFE, D.A. 1962. *Plant communities of the Scottish Highlands: a study of Scottish mountain, moorland and forest vegetation*. London: HMSO.

PFITZENMEYER, C.D.C. 1962. *Arrhenatherum elatius* (L.) J. & C. Presl. *Biol. Flora Br. Isl.*, no. 81.

SARGENT, CAROLINE & MOUNTFORD, J.O. 1980. *Biological survey of British Rail property. Fourth interim report.* (CST report no. 293). Banbury: Nature Conservancy Council.

SARGENT, CAROLINE & MOUNTFORD, J.O. 1981. *Biological survey of British Rail property. Fifth interim report.* (CST report no. 325). Banbury: Nature Conservancy Council.

WAY, J.M., MOUNTFORD, J.O. & SHEAIL, J. 1978. *British Rail land - biological survey. Second interim report.* (CST report no. 178). Banbury: Nature Conservancy Council.

AERIAL PHOTOGRAPHS AS RECORDS OF CHANGING VEGETATION PATTERNS

R M FULLER

Institute of Terrestrial Ecology, Monks Wood Experimental Station, Huntingdon

ABSTRACT

Aerial photographs provide baseline data on vegetation for monitoring subsequent changes, and may form a unique historical record of vegetation patterns. In using historical photographs to measure change, the ecologist has to be aware of the problems of interpretation and the difficulties caused by distortions, which may restrict the methodology used and the accuracy achieved; but, as long as the errors can be shown to be small in relation to the changes observed, valuable results can be obtained.

Some of the solutions to the problems are illustrated, by reference to a number of studies, with particular emphasis on techniques that can be applied by ecologists, often with limited resources, and with little training in photogrammetry.

INTRODUCTION

Plants establish, grow and die, so that even the most stable ecosystem is, in fact, dynamic, with measurable changes in time. In addition, man has continually reshaped the landscape, and a true climax vegetation is almost unknown in Britain. We can all tell of areas where the countryside of childhood memories has changed, almost beyond recognition. Yet can we give an accurate, let alone objective, account of what those changes have been? If ecologists are to advise on environmental management, to predict the results of developments, or assess the impacts of past activities, it is essential that they understand, and can communicate the nature, causes and extent of changing vegetation patterns.

Aerial photographs provide one of the most detailed and comprehensive records of changing vegetation cover, in Britain, over the last half century. They extend back to the 1920s (Howard 1970; St Joseph 1977) and cover, well, the period from about 1945 to the present. The quality of the early photographs, in terms of definition, is often as good as that of modern photographs, and the scales are usually compatible with mapping and measurement of plant communities. They may provide evidence of long term changes which can be studied within the duration of short term projects. Perhaps most importantly, the evidence is preserved for all to see and assess for themselves.

SOURCES OF PHOTOGRAPHS

Many of the early aerial photographs were taken by the Royal Air Force (RAF) but those taken before 1945 are relatively scarce and not fully catalogued. From 1945 onwards, the UK Town and County Planning Departments agreed free access to RAF aerial photographs with the Air Ministry. The Air Photographs Units of the Department of the Environment, the Welsh Office and the Scottish Development Department now maintain collections of early RAF material, Ordnance Survey (OS) material over 10 years old, and hold details of more recent OS, RAF and commercial sorties (Brotchie 1979). OS hold their recent cover at Southampton and other organizations, such as the Cambridge University Committee for Aerial Photography, maintain collections of their own prints. Keele University have a unique collection of prints covering western Europe, but not the UK, taken between 1939 and 1945. Local authorities may often commission, or know of the existence of aerial cover of their area. Unfortunately, systematic large scale coverage of the UK has apparently declined in recent years. In 1964 the Air Ministry decided that the RAF could no longer accept a planned flying programme (Brotchie 1979). Since then, OS has undertaken a programme of major revision involving photography, mainly in the early 1970s. But future large scale re-surveys seem likely to be piecemeal. RAF have covered the country at 1:50 000 in 1980/81. Landsat and other space imagery may fill some of the gaps. However, photography at scales between 1:2500 and 1:20 000 will remain an important source of data for ecologists.

TYPES OF PHOTOGRAPHY

The earliest prints generally available are oblique views, made by organizations such as Aerofilms. Most 1945-64 cover was taken by the RAF using the split-vertical, or split-pair format, where 2 parallel runs of photographs were taken simultaneously, using 2 cameras, one inclined to the left, one to the right of the flight run, at between 10° and 15° to the vertical: full stereoscopic cover gives the normal 3-dimensional model when overlapping prints are viewed with a stereoscope. Split-verticals can usually be recognized by the fact that they are 165 x 215 mm ($6\frac{1}{2}$ x $8\frac{1}{2}$ inch) instead of the now more usual 230 x 230 mm (9 x 9 inch) (Sewell 1966); often F21 or F22 is marked in the margin indicating that a fan of 2 cameras was used and that a print is from camera 1 or 2 respectively. Sometimes a 5-camera system was used, as may be evident from the F41-44 classification, with a simultaneous V or Vertical run. From the mid 1960s, most 'vertical' aerial photographs in the UK were taken with the camera axis tilted by no more than 3°.

PROBLEMS OF USING HISTORICAL AERIAL PHOTOGRAPHS

Firth (1973) points out that much of the work done with aerial photographs has been unsatisfactory, because the people who used them were unfamiliar with the nature of the material they were handling. Few ecologists have had formal instruction in the use of photographs, as part of their training in the methods of surveying vegetation. So, although nearly all British ecologists will have looked at photographs of their study sites, perhaps published sketch maps made from them to illustrate papers, or maybe used them to help stratify a sampling programme, in practice ecologists have made surprisingly little use of the detailed information that aerial photographs can provide (Goodier 1971); this would seem to remain the case in a recent survey of remote sensing users (Lindsay 1981). This is not because vegetation patterns show badly on aerial photographs, for photographs are frequently used in forestry, while soil scientists and archaeologists, for example, rely heavily upon differences in vegetation patterns to enhance the features that they seek to identify from aerial photographs (St Joseph 1977).

Too many published accounts of aerial mapping, in ecology textbooks, place emphasis on the advantages of different films and filters, of non-photographic sensing, of changing season and scale, without giving enough detail to allow ecologists to successfully use photographs already in existence. With financial constraints on research it is common to rely upon existing material rather than to commission new surveys. Furthermore, when commissioning a survey, such advice should be available from the survey company. One important textbook *Aerial photo-ecology* by Howard (1970) covers both theory and practice but needs updating with information on new equipment available. Also, the book makes little mention of the use of historical photographs and the special problems involved with them.

In using the perspective view provided by aerial photographs, allowance must be made for displacements, and the distortion of scale caused by tilts of the camera, or relief on the ground. The large scale foreground and small scale view into the distance, compressed into the frame of a high angle oblique photograph, is just an extreme example of the sort of distortions encountered with any tilted photograph. The way in which tall buildings and trees 'lean' away from the centre of a print just illustrates how high levels of relief can cause displacements on the photograph, as well as producing varying scales with points at varying distances from the camera. Maps made from uncorrected photographs are not likely to be accurate but people read maps as if they were without any error: yet, even OS maps are subject to errors (Harley 1975). Anyone using aerial photographs to map or measure a changing landscape should be confident that the changes observed are greater than the likely errors attributable to the methodology.

The large angles of tilt on some historical photographs, combined with the usual problems of relief displacement, may be further complicated by lens distortions and print shrinkage. Images may also have been lost or partially obscured by cloud cover, shadow, haze and reflected glare. Some photographs were taken with only minimal overlap and it is not possible to work in stereo; or the interval between frames was set wrongly and only perhaps 40% overlap was achieved giving runs of alternating stereo and mono blocks. The reaction might be to discard poor quality photographs; but, if they alone show the information required, then it should be possible to make use of them. Versatile methods of aerial photo-mapping may be needed to cope with such problems which arise all too frequently in historical studies.

In using historical aerial photographs it is not, of course, possible to verify the results of the subjective processes of photo-interpretation by conventional ground truth survey. But it is usually possible to find corroborative evidence in the field or in documents. And, of course, the photographs remain as, perhaps, the best check on the historical ecologist's interpretation.

THE GEOMETRY OF PERSPECTIVE VIEW PHOTOGRAPHS

Many accounts of the geometry of aerial photographs are available in photogrammetric textbooks (Born 1966; Tewinkel 1966; Howard 1970; Kilford 1973; Wolf 1974; Lo 1976), so it will suffice to mention only the conclusions here.

The scale of an aerial photograph is determined basically by the focal length of the camera lens and the flying height of the aircraft. If a feature is higher or lower than the datum set for determining flying height, then it will be at a larger or smaller scale than the surrounding land (Figure 1). The scale of a vertical photograph is given by:-

$$S = \frac{f}{H - h}$$

where:

S = scale

f = focal length

H = flying height

h = height of an object above datum

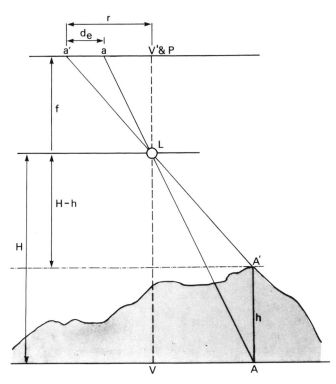

Figure 1   Photographic image displacement caused by relief variation

f – *focal length of camera*

H – *flying height*

h – *height of A' above datum*

A – *vertical projection of 'A' onto the datum plane*

L – *camera lens*

P – *principal point*

V – *nadir point*

V' – *image of V on negative*

d_e – *displacement of a' (image of A') from a (its planimetrically correct position)*

An object above the datum will also appear to be displaced from the centre of the photograph; in fact, it is displaced from the nadir point, which is the point where a plumb line through the perspective centre would meet the photograph (Figure 1). The amount of displacement is given by:-

$$d_e = \frac{rh}{H} \quad \text{(for a vertical photograph)}$$

where:

d_e = displacement

r = distance from the nadir point

This displacement may be used profitably in calculating heights, for example of topographic features, buildings or trees.

Tilt also causes scale distortions and displacements, in this case from the isocentre, a point midway between the nadir point and the principal point or centre of the photograph (Figure 2).

Tilt displacement is given by:-

$$d_t = \frac{y^2}{(f/\sin t)-y}$$

where:

d_t = displacement of point due to tilt

y = distance from isocentre to the point

t^{o} = angle of tilt

The scale of an image on a tilted photograph is given by:-

$$S = \frac{f - (y\ \sin\ t)}{H - h}$$

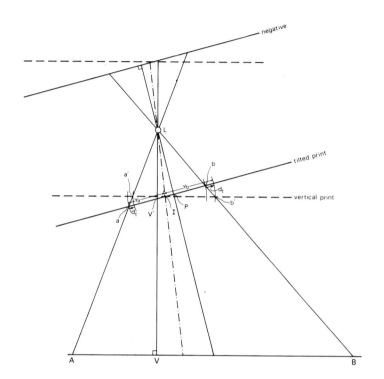

L   – *camera lens*

P   – *principal point*

V   – *nadir point*

V'   – *image of V*

I   – *isocentre*

a', b' – *images of ground features A and B*

d$_t$ – *displacement due to tilt of a and b (tilted images of A and B) from their planimetrically correct position*

Figure 2   Photographic image displacement caused by a tilted camera axis

Lens distortions and print shrinkage are small sources of error where metric aerial cameras have been used; so from a knowledge of the flying height, lens focal length, relief variation, maximum likely tilt and extent of the photographic area to be mapped, it is possible to calculate, approximately, the maximum likely levels of error involved, firstly, in placing features and, secondly, in scaling features, if maps are produced from photographs without applying correction for distortion.

RAF split verticals were generally taken with 508 mm (20 inch) lenses, long compared with the 152 mm (6 inch) lenses more commonly used now on metric mapping cameras (Sewell 1966). This means that the flying height is greater, for any given scale, making relief variation a smaller problem than it would be with a shorter lens; also,the tilt required to achieve 5-10% side lap is reduced. However, 10-15° of tilt is still needed at typical scales of around 1:10 000. High flight also means that the stereomodel, seen when adjacent pairs of photographs are viewed stereoscopically, is less exaggerated than that of modern photographs, making textural patterns a little less distinct in stereo and relief a little less obvious. In practice, though, this is rarely a problem. The need to correct for distortions caused by tilt, relief variation, film or print shrinkage and lens distortions depends upon the uses to which photographs are put.

THE PRACTICAL USE OF AERIAL PHOTOGRAPHS

Aerial photographs may be used simply for qualitative purposes, for inventory and for linear, areal or volumetric measurements.

Inventory

A search for signs of plant disease (Risbeth 1977) may involve no measurement on the photographs, and,therefore, no correction for distortion. Counting trees or animals can be done from oblique photographs without correction, just as long as the oblique view does not allow the objects of interest to 'hide' behind taller features. Peterken and Hubbard (1972) used photographs taken in 1939, 1942, 1962 and 1967 to follow changes in the populations of holly trees growing on shingle at Dungeness, Kent. Aerial photographs have commonly been used for forest inventories (Howard 1970) and census of large animals (Perkins 1971; Vaughan 1971; Milton & Darling 1977).

Linear measurements

Linear measurements over short distances on photographs can be made just with local correction to scale; width of ditches, diameters of bushes are examples. Over long distances, the image of a linear feature may significantly change in scale along its length and allowances must be made for this. Pollard *et al.* (1974) measured hedgerow losses using 1946 and 1962/63 aerial photographs, plus ground survey. As hedges appear as boundaries on OS maps, presence-or-absence information was transferred from photographs to existing maps, later to be measured accurately from those maps (Hooper personal communication).

Simple areal measurements

Measurements of area, if made without correction, will be subject to a greater proportional error than linear measurements. So more careful corrections may need to be made where areas are to be calculated. The equations given earlier allow a user to make an assessment of the potential errors. Again, a distinction can be made between small features, where scale distortions within may be considered uniform, and larger areas where they vary across a feature. Where errors require correction, various methods are available.

In a study that the Institute of Terrestrial Ecology (ITE) has just started, on drainage and land use on the Romney marshes, field types can be discerned on 1946 aerial photographs. The field boundaries, as shown on the OS 1:10 560 map (revised 1930-45), remained largely unchanged in 1946. In order to map land use it was generally only necessary to add the information on field types to the map, before measurements were made. Essentially the photo-interpretation was qualitative, with only occasional need to record the position of new boundaries.

Monoscopic transfer methods

Usually the ecologist will wish to add vegetation boundaries, of his own interpretation, to the boundaries and other features shown on existing OS maps. If this is the case, more sophisticated techniques are needed. But as Maling (1971) states, this is still really a revision of existing maps, in a rather specialized way. OS maps will usually form a suitable base of known accuracy. Built-up areas are mapped at 1:1250; most others are 1:2500,with mountain and moorland covered at 1:10 000 or 1:10 560 (Harley 1975).

A very simple method of transferring photographic detail on to OS maps is to project the image of the photograph, or a tracing of information made from it, on to the OS map; the image is enlarged or reduced to match the scales of the map. Hubbard (1965) mapped cord grass (*Spartina* spp.) invasion in Poole Harbour, Dorset, from 1924 and 1952 photographs fitted to the 1925 OS 1:10 560 map, using fixed points along the shore and photographic reduction to match the scales.

I have used a *Grant Projector* on various occasions to transfer details, which were traced under the stereoscope, of vegetation on flat coastal and wetland areas. This instrument allows the projected image to be reduced down to $\frac{1}{4}$x or enlarged up to 4x, but makes no correction for tilt. By fitting small areas of detail to local OS map features, it is possible for the operator to vary the enlargement factor as he works across a print, so compensating for scale changes caused by tilt. Using this method, paths were surveyed on the dunes at Winterton, the study backed up with ground surveys of the path networks (Boorman & Fuller 1977). The spread of *Rhododendron ponticum* on this site was studied using 1946, 1953 and 1973 aerial photographs at 1:12 00C, 1:5000 and 1:2500 respectively, and a ground survey made in 1972 (Fuller & Boorman 1977). Although no estimates of error were made, the 1946 dune photographs clearly showed very few bushes; by 1953 they covered 0.6 ha of dune, and by 1972 had spread to occupy *c*. 5.6 ha. Such changes could clearly not be explained in terms of mapping errors.

Reedswamp die-back in the Norfolk Broads was studied, under contract, for the Nature Conservancy Council (Boorman *et al*. 1979). Reed species, growing in water, were interpreted from aerial photographs viewed under the mirror stereoscope, and the outlines traced on to clear acetate overlays using a 0.15 mm pen with etching ink. Control points were also marked on to the acetate tracings; the same points were taken from OS 1:2500 sheets and marked on to a matt tracing film. The Grant Projector was then used to correct the scales of the acetate tracings, by projecting the information on to the film. By fitting detail locally, tilted images were corrected and transferred with reasonably accuracy. Eighteen Broads were mapped, representing 82% of the total water area of *c*. 35 Broads shown on OS 1:50 000 maps (excluding Breydon Water). For every site at least 4 sorties of vertical photographs were found, with 8 available at one. A total of 80 maps was produced from prints representing 47 films of vertical photographs. Also, 19 oblique flights provided checks on interpretation. It was possible to check some results against published data on Broadland vegetation.

The consistency of values for the total area (water plus reedswamp) of each Broad over the years 1945-1977 gave an indication of mapping accuracy. These values may have fluctuated because of real changes or because of errors (or a combination of both). In no case was the fluctuation greater than ±4% of the mean area. In the 6 Broads, where 6 or more maps were made. the differences in total area never exceeded ±1.5% ($P < 0.05$). As the reedswamp-to-water boundary was more clearly discernible than the land-to-reedswamp boundary, the values calculated for reedswamp are believed to be as accurate as those for total water area.

Photographic data were supplemented with OS map data; the results showed that losses, by die-back to open water, had been greatest at some time in the period between 1946 and 1963, minimal between 1963 and 1970, and had increased again from 1970-1977. This seemed to be related to periods of high coypu numbers (Boorman & Fuller 1981). Coypus, large South American rodents of wetland areas, had been released from fur farms in the 1930s, and populations had apparently grown exponentially in Broadland (Figure 3). However, the cold winters of 1946-47 and 1962-63 had reduced numbers drastically, and through the period 1963-70 a combination of trapping and cold winters had kept numbers down. From population and food intake figures supplied by L M Gosling of the Ministry of Agriculture, Fisheries and Food's Coypu Research Laboratory (personal communication), we were able to calculate the likely food intake of the animals during the period from 1930 to 1977. The total biomass of reed lost represented about 27% of the coypu food intake in that time. By modelling the effect of coypu taking reed as 27% of their diet, values being calculated year by year, a predicted decline curve was calculated (Boorman & Fuller 1981). This compared closely to actual values measured from aerial photographs (Figure 3).

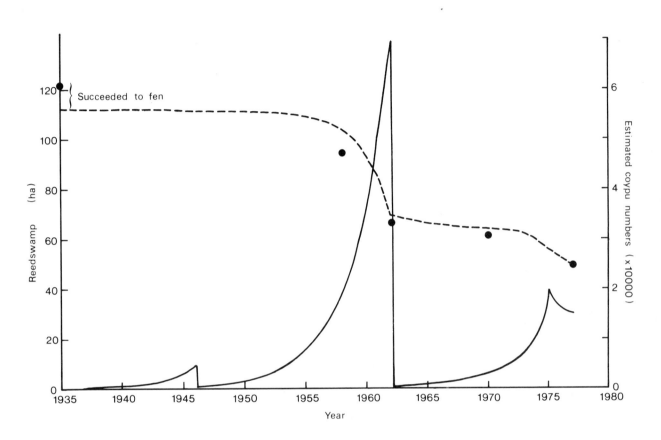

Figure 3   Changing coypu population (————) and reedswamp areas (1935–1977) as measured from aerial photographs (●) and as predicted with coypu taking reedswamp as 27% of their diet (– – –)

The use of this very simple method for mapping reedswamp had been very successful. However, we were only identifying 2 basic habitats, open water and reedswamp; and reedswamp only consisted of 2 major species *Phragmites australis* and *Typha augustifolia*. Being marginal vegetation, relief was non-existent, and the degree of change observed was so marked that great accuracy was unnecessary. But it should be realized that the Grant Projector has inherently bad optical qualities and that the method of correction is unsophisticated, and dependent very much on the skill of the operator. Other similar instruments such as the *Rost Plant Variograph* are optically better but expensive for the level of correction they offer.

Most transfer instruments allow some correction for tilt, and details are provided by P e nn ing ton (1966) with further and more recent detail given by Wolf (1974) and Lo (1976). Instruments based on the *camera lucida* principle are common. The *Vertical Sketchmaster* (by Aero Service Corporation) and the *Aero-Sketchmaster* (by Zeiss Aero-topograph) are examples of such instruments. When using a Sketchmaster, the operator sees the map to be revised through a double prism, superimposed on the aerial photograph. Map and/or photograph magnifications can be altered to match scales, and the photo-holder can be angled and rotated to eliminate some of the effects of tilt. But Maling (1971) suggests that it is a difficult instrument to use.

Another far more sophisticated example of a mono-scopic transfer instrument is the *Bausch and Lomb Zoom Transfer Scope (ZTS)*. Working on a similar principle, it provides a zoom control to magnify or reduce the photograph to match the base map. An optical stretch facility can be used to provide an equal and opposite distortion of the photograph to that caused by tilt and relief variation. McGivern *et al*. (1972) state that "..... the accuracy obtainable with the ZTS can meet (US) National Map Accuracy Standards".

Stereoscopic transfer methods

Photographs viewed under the stereoscope are much more easily interpreted; textures are enhanced, shadow penetration is improved, and clues to interpretation are more numerous. Furthermore, the effects of relief are readily appreciated, so that corrections can be applied more easily. Where an inadequate supply of control points exists, features of relief can be fitted to map contours.

Where stereoscopic viewing is needed to assist during interpretation, it is necessary, with monoscopic transfer instruments, to annotate the photographs using a conventional mirror stereoscope and, subsequently, transfer the details in a second stage of mapping; but stereoscopic transfer instruments are available.

The *Hilger and Watts Stereosketch* is a subjective projection instrument (Lo 1976) which provides stereo-viewing of paired photographs, together with a third image of the base map seen in one eye. Tilts of up to 5° (x and/or y) can be corrected, and photographic scale can be altered to accommodate 1:0.45 to 1:1.25, photo-to-drawing scale differences. Unfortunately, this is not a sufficient range to match all standard photographic scales with available OS maps. A new zoom version gives a range of 1:0.8 to 1:4.5 which overcomes this problem. However, the tilt correction range will not cope with split-vertical photographs.

The *Ottica-Meccanica Italiana (OMI) Stereo Facet Plotter* offers the range of corrections needed for most mapping tasks. It allows the user to see a pair of stereo photographs superimposed over a base map of known scale. By means of a mirror system, the map may be distorted to fit the photograph, a method which may lead to problems during the transfer. But the biggest problem is that enlargement of photographs is achieved by mounting the photographs on glass stages at varying heights above the upward facing viewing head, the result being that, on lower enlargements, the prints are so high above his head that the operator cannot reach them, to manoeuvre them whilst looking through the optical system to achieve stereoscopic registration. However, the Royal Commission on Historical Monuments have used the instrument successfully in archaeological studies (Hampton & Palmer 1977).

The *Bausch and Lomb Stereo-Zoom Transfer Scope (S-ZTS)* is an instrument with all the other features of the monoscopic ZTS, but with increased magnification and stereoscopic viewing. It is probably the most sophisticated of the pure transfer instruments available at present. The S-ZTS consists, basically, of a mirror stereoscope with a zoom magnifying head. Independent zoom adjustments for each print mean that differences in scale, arising from altitude changes between exposures, can be accommodated by independent adjustments. Photographs can be enlarged from 0.6x to 16x actual size and the map to 1x, 2x and 4x actual size, giving an excellent range of working scales.

Distortions of the photographic images, caused by tilt and relief variation,

can be corrected locally by providing equal and opposite distortion, on the
S-ZTS, using the stretch facility. Initial adjustments are made with the
instrument set in mono-mode but stereo can be selected and adjustments made
to zoom and stretch of the second image, to match it to the first.

The S-ZTS is being used to map 300 km^2 of Broadland vegetation under a
contract with the Broads Authority (BA), with Grant Aid from the Countryside
Commission. Sixteen natural and semi-natural habitats are mapped plus 15 other
land use classes, to provide 1:10 000 scale maps of the BA Executive Area.
Accuracy of interpretation is being checked using 1:2000 stereo colour transparencies of sample quadrats in Broadland. The maps are being digitized at
the Natural Environment Research Council (NERC)'s Experimental Cartography Unit
(ECU) (Fuller & Drummond 1981) to provide data files that are then used to
produce output maps, data on lengths and areas of features; finally, we have a
versatile data set that can be used for analysis of change, to test for relationships between the distributions of different vegetation types and factors such as
soil types, water quality, boat traffic densities or coypu populations.

The data are being made compatible with ECOBASE. This is a series of data
files of environmental variables generated by NERC at ECU. It consists of
digitized cartographic information on British hydrological and communication
networks, urban and forested areas. The data will also form an example of high
resolution data within the Terrestrial Environment Information System (TEIS)
being developed at ITE Bangor as a result of projects on ecological mapping and
described in this symposium (Ball *et al.*; Bunce *et al.*; Sargent). Parry (in
press) has used the S-ZTS in studies of historical changes in the extent of
moorland in the National Parks of England and Wales. They used, for example,
1953, 1966 and 1968 photographs and OS maps to follow the history of land reclamation and reversion in the Peak District, successfully coping with the
problems of relief variation and large tilts, simultaneously.

Photogrammetric plotting

So far in this paper I have mentioned approximate techniques of transfer
for subjective correction of the distortions of the aerial photograph. Conventional photogrammetry and analytical plotting both have an important place in
ecological mapping. Other papers in this symposium, by R Fenton and I Dowman,
make more mention of these techniques so I will not go into any detail on them.
But I will make several points. First, some of these techniques will not cope
with the large tilts found on split-vertical and oblique photographs. Secondly,
few instruments will take prints, so new transparencies may have to be made.
Thirdly, most rely upon the presence of full stereo coverage to make their
transformations. Fourthly, they are techniques which are not suitable for use
by untrained personnel. So ecologists wishing to use photogrammetric plotting
techniques will either have to put in a large amount of effort in learning the
methodology, or will be contracting the work out to another organization. This
may often be the most appropriate way of making maps of unsurveyed areas, where
transfer techniques cannot be applied, or for making maps at higher levels of
accuracy. And although topographic maps can theoretically be made on a number
of transfer instruments using floating spot lighting devices, the plotting
machine or analytical plotter is more appropriate for this work.

CONCLUSION

The most important thing for the ecologist to remember is that, whatever
method is used to map and measure from aerial photographs, an assessment of
potential errors must be made if a sound analysis is to result from their use
as records of changing vegetation patterns.

REFERENCES

BOORMAN, L.A. & FULLER, R.M. 1977. Studies on the impact of paths on the dune vegetation at Winterton, Norfolk, England. *Biol. Conserv.*, 12, 203-216.

BOORMAN, L.A. & FULLER, R.M. 1981. The changing status of reedswamp in the Norfolk Broads. *J. appl. Ecol.*, 18, 241-269.

BOORMAN, L.A., FULLER, R.M. & BOAR, R.R. 1979. *Recent changes in the distribution of reedswamp in Broadland.* (CST report no. 267). Banbury: Nature Conservancy Council.

BORN, C.J. 1966. Mechanical methods of phototriangulation. In: *Manual of photogrammetry*, edited by M.M. Thompson, R.C. Eller, W.A. Radlinski and J.L. Speert, 377-459. 3rd ed. Falls Church, Va: American Society of Photogrammetry.

BROTCHIE, A.W. 1979. The use of remote sensing by the Scottish Development Department. In: *Environmental monitoring by remote sensing*, edited by P.A. Vass. London: Remote Sensing Society.

FIRTH, J.G. 1973. The aerial photograph - not a map yet more than a map. *Scott. For.*, 27, 336-344.

FULLER, R.M. & BOORMAN, L.A. 1977. The spread and development of *Rhododendron ponticum* L. on dunes at Winterton, Norfolk, in comparison with invasion by *Hippophae rhamnoides* L. at Saltfleetby, Lincolnshire. *Biol. Conserv.*, 12, 83-94

FULLER, R.M. & DRUMMOND, J.E. 1981. Photointerpretation and computer aided cartography of Broadland vegetation. In: *Matching remote sensing technologies and their applications. Proc. Ann. Conf. Remote Sens. Soc., 9th, London, 1981*, 347-358. Reading: University of Reading, Remote Sensing Society.

GOODIER, R., ed. 1971. *The application of aerial photography to the work of the Nature Conservancy.* Edinburgh: Nature Conservancy.

HAMPTON, J.N. & PALMER, R. 1977. Implications of aerial photography for archaeology. *Archaeol. J.*, 134, 157-193.

HARLEY, J.B. 1975. *Ordnance Survey maps: a descriptive manual.* Southampton: Ordnance Survey.

HOWARD, J.A. 1970. *Aerial photo-ecology.* London: Faber & Faber.

HUBBARD, J.C.E. 1975. *Spartina* marshes in southern England: VI Pattern of invasion in Poole Harbour. *J. Ecol.*, 53, 799-813.

KILFORD, W.J. 1973. *Elementary air survey.* 3rd ed. London: Pitman.

LINDSAY, E.J. 1981. *Remote sensing of earth resources.* 5th ed. London: Department of Industry.

LO, C.P. 1976. *Geographical applications of aerial photography.* London: David & Charles.

MALING, D.H. 1971. Photogrammetric techniques relevant to the Nature Conservancy's use of air photography. In: *The application of aerial photography to the work of the Nature Conservancy*, edited by R. Goodier, 132-149. Edinburgh: Nature Conservancy.

McGIVERN, R., MARTIN, D. & BENJAMIN, J. 1972. Planimetric map revision with the Bausch & Lomb Zoom Transfer Scope. *Proc. Ann. Mtg American Society of Photogrammetry, 38th, 1972*, 615-616.

MILTON, J. & DARLING, SIR F.F. 1977. Aerial photography and zoology. In: *The uses of air photography*, edited by J.K.S. St Joseph, 114-123. 2nd ed. London: John Baker.

PARRY, M. in press. *Surveys of moorland and roughland change. 3: Airphoto mapping of moorland and roughland change.* Birmingham: University of Birmingham.

PENNINGTON, J.T. 1966. Paper print plotters. In: *Manual of Photogrammetry*, edited by M.M. Thompson, R.C. Eller, W.A. Radlinski and J.L. Speert, 537-556. 3rd ed. Falls Church, Va: American Society of Photogrammetry.

PERKINS, D.F. 1971. The Dartmoor survey. In: *The application of aerial photography to the work of the Nature Conservancy*, edited by R. Goodier, 78-87. Edinburgh: Nature Conservancy.

PETERKEN, G.F. & HUBBARD, J.C.E. 1972. The shingle vegetation of southern England: the hollywood on Holmestone beach, Dungeness. *J. Ecol.*, 60, 547-571.

POLLARD, E., HOOPER, M.D. & MOORE, N.W. 1974. *Hedges.* London: Collins.

RISBETH, J. 1977. Air photography and plant disease. In: *The uses of air photography*, edited by J.K.S. St Joseph, 103-111. 2nd ed. London: John Baker.

ST JOSEPH, J.K.S. 1977. *The uses of air photography.* 2nd ed. London: John
    Baker.
SEWELL, E.D. 1966. Aerial cameras. In: *Manual of photogrammetry,* edited bv M.M.
    Thompson, R.C. Eller, W.A. Radlinski and J.L. Speert, 133-194. 3rd ed.
    Falls Church, Va: American Society of Photogrammetry.
TEWINKEL, G.C. 1966. Basic mathematics of photogrammetry. In: *Manual of photo-*
    grammetry, edited by M.M. Thompson, R.C. Eller, W.A. Radlinski and J.L. Speert,
    17-65. 3rd ed. Falls Church, Va: American Society of Photogrammetry.
VAUGHAN, R.W. 1971. Aerial photography in seals research. In: *The application of*
    aerial photography to the work of the Nature Conservancy, edited by R. Goodier,
    88-98. Edinburgh: Nature Conservancy.
WOLF, P.R. 1974. *Elements of photogrammetry.* New York, London: McGraw-Hill.

THE USE OF PHOTOGRAMMETRIC TECHNIQUES IN NATURE CONSERVATION

R A FENTON
Nature Conservancy Council, Taunton

ABSTRACT

In a country so apparently well mapped as Great Britain it should not be necessary for small organizations such as the Institute of Terrestrial Ecology and the Nature Conservancy Council to devote much time, effort and finance in producing their own detailed maps. Sadly, experience has shown that to prepare sophisticated maps and inventories at scales of 1:10 000 and upwards it is essential to invest in a comparatively wide range of equipment and skills. During the past 32 years, first the Nature Conservancy and, latterly, the Nature Conservancy Council have found it necessary to employ a range of photogrammetric techniques to produce the maps and plans needed for ecological mapping. Experience has shown that, to obtain the best maps at the most economical cost, it is necessary to both produce work inhouse and, on occasion, commission it from commercial or academic sources. Details are provided of the equipment, services and costs of surveys and maps used by the Council.

INTRODUCTION

The German polymath, Alexander von Humboldt (1769-1859) once said "The best map is a blank sheet of paper"; this sounds rather a silly statement until one considers the mapping requirements of an explorer like Humboldt, and specialists such as those employed in organizations like the Institute of Terrestrial Ecology (ITE) and the Nature Conservancy Council (NCC). For Humboldt's statement should be pondered when one considers that in Great Britain alone there are currently nearly 30 publicly funded agencies who have acquired and are using major items of photogrammetric equipment to produce their own specialized maps. These organizations range from departments like the Ordnance Survey (OS) and the Directorate of Overseas Surveys, to the NCC and the Photogrammetric Unit of the Institute of Advanced Architectural Studies at the University of York. Additionally, there are some 20 commercial firms specializing in supplying photogrammetrically produced surveys to a wide range of government departments and private firms; and Wiltshire County Council has even found it pays to have its own plotting machine (a Wild B8) for revising OS 1:1000 and 1:2500 mapping of its towns and villages, and for contouring some 788 km^2 of the county at a 2 m vertical interval (Anon 1980).

This considerable outlay of public and private funds indicates that many organizations, in spite of having access to all the OS large and medium scale surveys (including Supply of Unpublished Survey Information), find that there is still a large gap left in the nation's mapping which has had to be filled by the purchase and use of a very large range of complex photogrammetric equipment. Further, the expenditure does not stop at photogrammetric plotting machines, because it is also necessary to have sophisticated topographic survey equipment in order to supply the planimetric control for all this photogrammetry and, of course, large sums of money have to be spent in acquiring aerial photography, which is in itself a very expensive procedure as a new metric air survey camera can cost up to £100,000 by the time all the relevant back-up equipment has been acquired. Clearly this expensive dichotomy did not come about at the whim of a few people; rather, those responsible for the development of the country's resources were forced to commission large scale surveys simply because the OS, with the limited resources available to it, could not produce quickly enough the maps and plans required, in sufficient numbers and at the requisite scales.

HISTORICAL PERSPECTIVES

To discover how this situation came about, one must go back to the late 1930s, for by then the 1:2500 County Series mapping had fallen into such a parlous state that it was necessary to appoint a Committee of Enquiry to investigate the problems facing the OS and to recommend a course of action which would restructure the country's large scale map series. The Davidson Committee, as it was known, reported in 1938 and made a series of wide ranging proposals, the main ones being that the country's maps should be based upon one Central Meridian (rather than on clusters of them), that these maps should be based upon a National Grid system, and that the old County Series plans should be 'overhauled' and cast in a national series of sheets, which would be revised to an acceptable level of accuracy as quickly and as cheaply as possible. The Davidson Committee also recommended that the possibility of mapping urban areas at 1:1250 (50" to 1 mile) should be investigated. Sadly, of course, the 1939–45 war took place so that these sensible proposals could not be acted upon at once, although some experimental surveys at 1:2500 and 1:1250 took place in the Bournemouth area in 1944. After the war it was necessary, because of the extensive areas laid waste by enemy action, to concentrate upon remapping urban Britain as quickly as possible in order to provide a basis for planning development in a coherent manner. The OS was called upon to produce a national series of 51 694, 1:1250 plans covering about 5.7% of Great Britain (Harley 1975), which meant that the long overdue revamping of the 1:2500 County Series plans had to be phased over a period of 35 or so years.

This was particularly trying for any organization needing large scale mapping of rural Britain because, particularly in the 1950s and early 1960s, the revision work of the OS was, of necessity, concentrated in lowland Britain. Consequently, in the early days of the Nature Conservancy (NC)'s reserve acquisition programme, almost all the maps used dated from around the 1920s and frequently back into the first decade of the century. Further, as the plans were overhauled rather than resurveyed, they were prone to minor inaccuracies and distortions because of frequent revisions and because of the need to change a County Meridian to a National Meridian. Tests have shown the order of accuracy of this series to be ± 2.5 m (Harley 1975) which is, of course, not a critically significant amount, but nonetheless is quite large enough when one is using Electronic Distance Measuring (EDM) equipment, which is accurate to within ± 1 cm in a km, and there can be minor frustrations when trying to tie new detail into old.

A further considerable drawback is the fact that the overhauled 1:2500 series does not cover the whole country and there are extensive areas where the largest scale map available is the OS 1:10 000 series and it is, of course, in just such areas that many of our National Nature Reserves (NNRs) fall – Rhum, Cairngorms, etc – with many other reserves only partially covered by 1:2500 mapping.

In themselves, these factors – outdatedness, minor directional inaccuracies and partial or no cover at all – were not crucial, and we made the best use we could of the available maps, but there was one further factor which eventually forced us to look elsewhere for much of our large scale mapping, and this was the paucity of topographical detail appearing on large scale plans. The maps were excellent in showing man-made features but, where sheets comprised only natural features, there was a distinct tendency to fill them with a mass of symbols, and this same approach carried over from the County Series plans to the new 1:2500 'overhaul' maps. Yet it was the natural features which were so very important to the NC when preparing and executing its management plans. This problem applied especially to coastal areas such as marshes and dunes, and also to upland and peatland sites.

The first time I encountered this problem was in 1959 at Braunton Burrows, where, in the late 1950s, the Coastal Physiographic Section was producing a series of detailed 1:2500 plans upon which to base further research and to record management work - the replanting of bare dunes with marram, establishment of brushwood fences, changes in dune configuration, etc; and to this end the Section laboriously plane-tabled the whole of the Burrows over a 5 year period. Even in 1955 such methods were something of an anachronism, but lack of funds and of good quality aerial photographs dictated these less efficient methods. Thus, by 1959 the NC was faced with the need to utilize photogrammetric techniques if it were to cope with the mapping tasks it would have to undertake in the next decade, but funds then, as now, were short and, when faced with the need to update its field survey equipment, invest in a second order plotting machine and commission large amounts of good quality aerial photography, the organization felt unable to underwrite such a programme, and had to search around for an alternative.

SURVEYS BY UNIVERSITIES

Fortunately it was at about this time (the early 1960s) that all the hard work by photogrammetrists in the university world began to bear fruit, for by then there were several well equipped departments - notably University College London (UCL), Glasgow and Swansea - each with funds for MSc research students. Thus, quite fortuitously for the NC, was born a series of research and mapping projects which, to some extent at least, solved the more serious mapping problems and, most importantly, set high standards for future work. At the same time, UCL generously gave 6 weeks' intensive plotting machine training to one of our cartographers, and, equally generously, Cambridge University allowed the NC to use its Wild B8 plotting machine upon which were produced 1:1000 scale maps of sites in upland Wales.

Clearly there were benefits to both parties; the universities were able to have access to viable, very demanding surveying and photogrammetric projects and the NC was able to get its maps at far below their true costs, and on this basis work has been carried out for us by 7 universities and 2 polytechnics.

The spread of mapping projects and techniques has been very diverse, ranging from large scale mapping of small sites to the medium scale mapping of individual NNRs as large as the Isle of Rhum. Some of the projects have been completed in a few months and others have gone on for several years, but in all cases the aim has been to find a genuine intellectual challenge, and many of the tasks have given students an exacting foretaste of planning and organizing major surveys, to the standard they would be expected to work to, on joining one of the major survey organizations. The commissioning and paying for work we place with universities tend to vary with almost every project. Some departments require us to underwrite the cost of aerial photography, purchase of OS trigonometric lists, cost of drafting materials, and so on. Other departments prefer to work to a contract which specifies unit costs, supervision drills, delivery dates, etc. The fact that we have been able to work in these ways for over 20 years demonstrates that there is much to be said for this joint approach between the universities and small departments such as the NCC and ITE.

It is almost unfair to single out any particular university but special mention should be made of the exceptionally high standard and breadth of work carried out for us by Professor Gordon Petrie's department in Glasgow. Starting with relatively small projects centring on Loch Lomond, work gradually expanded until in the late 1960s we jointly undertook the preparation of a completely new topographic map of Rhum, urgently needed by the NC, as at that time the extant

OS 1:10 560 sheets dated from the turn of the century. The new map was required as a base for R E C Ferreira's 21 community, vegetation survey (unpublished report held at NCC Inverness). Before work could begin on the vegetation map, a full 1:5000 scale photogrammetric survey was carried out using ground control, acquired over many months' field surveying, and completely new 1:10 000 aerial photography. In addition to the 1: 20 000 vegetation map, there also sprang a whole suite of maps - geomorphology, geology and topography at several scales.

PHOTOGRAMMETRY IN NCC

By the late 1960s, senior management accepted the need for the NC to have its own inhouse photogrammetric capacity and in 1970 we became owners of a Kern PG 2 L second order plotting machine purchased on the advice of our university contacts, and the Geography Department at University College of Wales, Swansea, kindly gave our photogrammetrist a fortnight's intensive tuition on the Department's own PG 2 L. Thus, for the past decade we have had our own plotting facility as well as those of the universities plus, on occasion, those of the commercial air survey organizat- ions. Sadly though, both the commercial and national mapping agencies have only rarely been able to figure in our photogrammetric and survey programmes because of the high costs involved, although we do whenever possible invite them to tender for large scale topographic surveys.

The advent of the pocket, programmable calculator, together with the new generation of lightweight EDM equipment, has had a remarkable impact on our survey productivity rates, for it is now possible to calculate National Grid co-ordinates in the field in minutes rather than the hours of earlier days. This facility is particularly useful when we have to set out new fence lines, drainage channels and experimental plots, as we can now give the man on the spot revised large scale plans with the proposed features plotted on them so that field staff and contrac- tors can be briefed immediately and work put in hand with the minimum delay. The NCC has 4 sets of EDM equipment; one set in each country maps office and one spare, first generation set, for use by field staff for carrying out minor survey work. This equipment is frequently used at distances well in excess of 1 km so our field parties are also equipped with 2-way handset radios - another expense which must be considered when setting up a survey/photogrammetric team.

Our present facilities offer us considerable flexibility and enable us to produce rapid machine plots for use at site meetings, or detailed plans for urgent management tasks. The Godlingston Heath extension to Studland Heath NNR is a case in point where the OS 1:10 000 map does not show the sort of detail which is so critical in managing the reserve, and we found it necessary to produce scale plans of topographic and land use detail, before acquisition of the reserve could proceed.

OTHER METHODS OF MAPPING

Obviously not all reserves lend themselves to photogrammetric plotting techniques - areas of dense wood and scrub will always present problems, partic- ularly if detailed heighting is required and on such occasions one can consider producing an orthophoto. This is a technique whereby the conventional air photo- graph is reconstituted in such a way that all the images appear in their true plan position; thus the photograph becomes a map. The instrumentation for bring- ing about this transformation is naturally very expensive and orthophotography is usually only commissioned by the larger public authorities and civil engineering organizations but, with an element of self help, costs can be brought to around £80 per overlap, provided one carries out the initial field survey work to establish the essential ground control needed for the later production stages.

There are also times when to use full blown photogrammetric techniques is both expensive and unnecessary; this applies particularly to the revision of medium scale mapping where good ground control already exists. The NCC frequently uses a Zeiss Sketchmaster to revise OS 1:10 000 scale mapping. Ideally the work should fall within areas of similar height and, although it can be used where the terrain ranges over 75 m or so, the equipment is at its best in revising coastal and marshland sites, and all the plotting for a new medium scale map of Scolt Head Island NNR was done on the Sketchmaster. A halfway house between the Sketchmaster and the second order plotting machine is the Bausch and Lomb Stereo-Zoom Transfer Scope which, providing good ground control exists, can be used for a wide range of map work. (See Fuller this symposium.)

A further valuable spinoff from using university departments to carry out agreed mapping tasks is that sometimes the final map is accompanied by a report detailing exactly how a task was carried out; we find this particularly useful because the knowledge gained can be incorporated into future, similar, tasks and frequently help to provide management prescriptions. An excellent example of this approach is Portsmouth Polytechnic's work on mapping the intertidal areas of Chichester Harbour (Budd & Coulson 1981). The survey was carried out as part of a contract issued by NCC's Chief Scientist's Team. The report covers all aspects of mapping the intertidal zone from commissioning the aerial photography, through the interpretative work, to the final mapping process. Another very useful report was Aberystwyth's assessment on the range of mapping techniques which could usefully be employed on a typical reserve, which gives descriptions of the various options available and their likely order of cost (Collin & Weir 1976).

MAPS AS PART OF MAJOR SURVEYS

To turn to some specific projects which point up some of the problems involved in mapping a wide variety of habitats, our work with Glasgow on the Rhum vegetation map has already been mentioned but this is only one of many. Another vegetation map was that covering Dartmoor which was very much a joint effort between the Geography Department of University College of Wales, Aberystwyth, and the NC, with inputs from many disciplines, the vegetation map being a contribution to the overall ecological work described by Perkins and Ward (1970). The final (1:63 360) map was a summary of all the detailed 1:10 560 scale plots produced from interpreting specially commissioned 1:10 000 scale colour and panchromatic aerial photography. Aerial photography at 1:2500 scale was also used for a series of transects across Dartmoor to carry out a census of animals grazing on the open moor and to study their distribution in relation to habitat, the results being recorded on OS 1:10 560 base maps. The project was not only of great value in assembling a large body of useful information about Dartmoor, it also offered valuable experience in carrying out a project with a wide range of contractors, which has been of great help in planning and co-ordinating later surveys.

Our inhouse photogrammetric work has, necessarily, had to be concentrated on providing rapidly produced large scale mapping for reserve acquisition and for management of the reserves once declared. Porton Down on the Wiltshire/Hampshire border is a case where it was essential that the NCC had 1:2500 maps to carry out detailed ecological survey work. The area, although not a reserve, is of great importance, being the largest continuous area of chalk grassland remaining in England. The area has been continuously occupied and used by the military authorities since it was requisitioned in 1916, before which much of the area was known to be arable land, and a large part of its previous history can be gleaned from historical records (Ratcliffe 1977).

Thus, there was much to be gained by mapping present day plant communities and seeking correlations with early data. To enable such comparisons to be made and to provide the essential large scale base maps, the PG 2 L plotting machine was used to prepare a series of 1:2500 plans. These sheets are a compromise between a straightforward topographical map and a detailed vegetation map and as such are useful both as a base map for management work and as a record of the main, visible vegetation communities.

On occasion, we have produced photogrammetric plots of portions of our reserves to serve as base maps for a particular piece of research we have either sponsored or are keen to see completed. A good example of this type of map work is at Axmouth/Lyme Regis Undercliffs NNR where a research student from Liverpool Polytechnic carried out work for a PhD thesis on the history of the landslips, their soils, geology and geomorphology, which will be of considerable value to the NCC when carrying out management work and further geomorphological studies on the reserve.

Mapping the landslips presented considerable problems, for the research student required very detailed large scale maps of small selected areas of the reserve which involved us in placing a series of markers and establishing their positions with great accuracy, as the markers were to be used as a baseline for further, long term measurements of any slippages which might take place. A series of 1:2500 plots was then prepared of the critical areas and some profiling was done on sequential sets of aerial photographs to quantify the amount of slipping which had taken place in a 10 year period.

TERRESTRIAL AND LOW LEVEL AERIAL PHOTOGRAMMETRY

As well as carrying out mapping from aerial photographs, the PG 2 can also be used for mapping from stereo ground photographs. This is a technique which we have used on occasion for mapping cliff faces, as an ordinary large scale plan does, of course, only depict the *plan* view, whereas our need is for detailed maps, in the vertical plane, for places such as the cliffs at Cwm Idwal and Craig y Cilau. Usually we get around this problem by commissioning either low level oblique air photographs or photographs taken on the ground, from which we then make up mosaics and produce dyeline copies from film positive transparencies for field use.

More rigorous mapping of such features is, of course, a practical proposition, for there are phototheodolites available to help provide the basic ground control needed when plotting on a photogrammetric plotter. At Coed Tremadog NNR in North Wales there have been problems caused by rock falls over many years, but in recent years these have been very worrying, particularly so since there was a severe rock fall in 1976 which damaged several adjacent houses. This led to the commissioning of a report on the state of the rock face by a firm of civil engineers. Rather than carry out a detailed large scale topographical survey, they chose instead to map the critical areas by photogrammetric techniques using a firm, Photarc, who specialize in this work. This firm supplied 2 1:200 scale plots of the rock face depicting all the unstable parts and these maps were used as the basis for planning and siting the remedial works. These plans are of great value to the NCC now, and they will continue to be, so that we can, without much trouble, update them on our own plotter.

CONCLUSIONS

In this brief survey of how the NCC has, over the years, made use of photogrammetric techniques, there is not space to cover all the work which has been done, but it does give an indication of how the organization obtains mapping. Nothing described is at all new or revolutionary, but it does show what can be done in a small department to make the fullest use of the resources available. There are hundreds more sites which need mapping in detail; we now need to match the interpretative and scientific skills of the ecologists to the skills and resources of the photogrammetrists, to produce a steady flow of high quality maps of critical areas, but we must avoid each group trying to do the other's job – a thing which has happened all too frequently in the past – quite enough wheels have been re-invented without ecologists and cartographers continuing the process!

REFERENCES

ANON. 1980. Report of the British National Committee for Photogrammetry.

BUDD, J.T.C. & COULSON, M.G. 1981. *Ecological mapping of the intertidal zone of Chichester Harbour*. (CST Report no. 353). Banbury: Nature Conservancy Council.

COLLIN, R.L. & WEIR, M.J.C. 1976. *A comparative assessment of some photogrammetric and cartographic options for mapping small nature reserves*. University College of Wales, Aberystwyth, unpublished report to the Nature Conservancy Council.

HARLEY, J.B. 1975. *Ordnance Survey maps: A descriptive manual*. Southampton: Ordnance Survey.

PERKINS, D.F. & WARD, S.D., eds. 1970. *Report on Dartmoor ecological survey, 1969*. Bangor: Nature Conservancy.

RATCLIFFE, D.A. 1977. *A nature conservation review: the selection of biological sites of national importance to nature conservation in Britain*. Vol. 2, 125-126. London: Cambridge University Press.

THE USE OF UNCONVENTIONAL PHOTOGRAPHS IN MAPPING

I J DOWMAN
Department of Photogrammetry and Surveying, University College London

ABSTRACT

Unconventional photography is defined as that which is not taken from an aircraft with a metric camera with near vertical axis. Whilst conventional photography is ideal for plotting topographical maps and large scale plans, there are many other applications when unconventional photography is more suitable. This paper describes the main characteristics of unconventional photography and then examines methods which are available for producing maps or co-ordinates, from them; these methods include fit and trace methods, numerical methods and use of analytical plotting instruments. The paper includes some examples of applications in which these methods have been used.

INTRODUCTION

Photogrammetry is concerned with obtaining quantitative information from photographs, and generally that means obtaining accurate measurements of features imaged on the photographs and placing those features in their correct position on a map. The most widespread use of photogrammetry - using aerial photography for making topographic maps and large scale plans - is exclusively concerned with photographs taken with virtually distortion-free cameras, and the plotting of accurate maps. A small number of photogrammetrists is also concerned with other types of photographs and other applications; these include the use of non-metric photography for medical and archaeological use and the use of digital imagery from space. The United Kingdom is currently responsible for Commission V of the International Society for Photogrammetry and Remote Sensing, which is concerned with Special Applications of Photogrammetry and Remote Sensing. The interest in geometry and the accuracy of the data are maintained in these applications, and it is this which distinguishes the photogrammetrist from the photointerpreter or remote sensor. This is not to say that the photogrammetrist is only interested in high accuracy; he often works with low tolerances, but is always aware of the accuracy with which he is working and of the geometry of the imagery and the method of restitution.

This paper is concerned with unconventional photography and by this is meant any photography which is not taken with a photogrammetric aerial camera with the camera axis almost vertical. Unconventional photography therefore includes all oblique photography and terrestrial photographs taken with a metric or non-metric camera; space imagery can also be included. This may seem a wide definition but it is useful because most photogrammetric plotting instruments are designed to accommodate near vertical aerial photographs and anything else has to be dealt with in an unconventional way. Frequently the accuracy required in measurement or plotting from unconventional photographs is less than that required from conventional photogrammetric procedures and, if that is so, the methods of restitution need not be so rigorous, and even quite simple methods can be used. The remainder of the paper will be concerned with the characteristics of unconventional photography, methods of restitution and some samples of applications.

CHARACTERISTICS OF UNCONVENTIONAL PHOTOGRAPHY

The 3 most common types of unconventional photography are terrestrial photographs taken with a metric camera, any non-metric photography and oblique photography. The first category does not usually give problems unless the photographs are also oblique, because such photography can be used on some plotting instruments and usually owners of the cameras have access to suitable plotting equipment such as the Wild B8 plotting instrument or the Kern PG 2. (See Fenton this symposium.)

The characteristics of non-metric photography include the presence of lens distortion, lack of film flatness and use of a focal plane shutter. All of these features disturb the normal perspective image obtained from a metric camera. In Figure 1, the ideal perspective geometry is shown and the angle of entry of a ray of light into the lens is equal to the angle of exit $\alpha = \alpha'$, the focal plane is flat and normal to the axis of the lens po and the whole image is exposed simultaneously. This latter condition may be obtained with a focal plane shutter if the film and the object remain in the same relative position to each other during exposure.

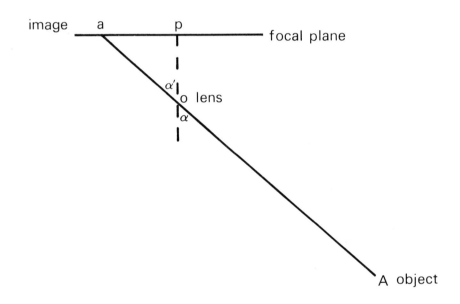

Figure 1   Normal perspective geometry of a light ray passing through a lens

In order to determine the position A in 3 dimensions from the image a, 2 photographs are needed and the positions of the principal point p and the principal distance po are required. If distortions due to the use of a non-metric camera are present, then allowance must be made for them. This cannot usually be done on a photogrammetric plotting instrument.

The image of A can be placed in its correct position relative to other points on a map if a projective transformation is used. This can be done without knowledge of the position of the principal point or principal distance and is the basis of several methods of plotting discussed later. The deformation of the image caused by different non-metric cameras varies but this can be reduced to insignificant amounts with suitable methods of correction.

Near vertical photographs have a strong resemblance to a map and plotting instruments are designed to correct tilts of up to 10° or so, depending on the instrument; photographs taken with camera axes horizontal and normal to the object photographed can also be treated in this way. Oblique photographs have large scale-changes across them and can only be dealt with in instruments which incorporate optical transformation elements.

Other types of image such as scanner imagery or panoramic photographs require special treatment. If the image is in digital form, such as Landsat multispectral scanner imagery, a transformation can be applied to produce a geometrically correct image.

METHODS OF PLOTTING FROM UNCONVENTIONAL PHOTOGRAPHS

The most straightforward and often the most satisfactory method of plotting detail from unconventional photography is using the method of fit and trace; this is based on the principle of projective transformation whereby any 2 plane quadrangles can be transformed one to the other. In practice it means distorting the photograph in some way so that details which are common to the photograph and a map or plotting sheet are made to correspond. Additional detail can then be traced on to the map. This method requires nothing more than a single photograph and a corresponding map or plot of control, and a suitable instrument. A limitation of the method is that no height information can be obtained and no correction can be made for sudden changes in relief.

A number of instruments are available, ranging from the long established reflecting plotter (or sketchmaster) which permits a projective transformation by tilting the photograph, through the Zoom Transfer Scope and the Facet Plotter which use anamorphic optics to distort the image, to very new microprocessor assisted instruments applying anamorphic corrections. Some of these instruments are listed in Table 1.

TABLE 1   Some simple instruments for plotting from unconventional photography

Manufacturer	Model	Description
Bausch and Lomb, Rochester, USA	Zoom Transfer Scope	Reflecting plotter type instrument incorporating variable magnification and anamorphic correction in optical system
	Stereo-Zoom Transfer Scope	As above, but with facility for 2 photographs
OMI, Rome, Italy	Stereo Facet Plotter	Similar to Stereo-Zoom Transfer Scope
Carl Zeiss Oberkochen, W Germany	Aero-Sketchmaster	Standard reflecting plotter

The accuracy of products from fit and trace methods will vary according to the nature of the original photograph, the amount of existing detail and control which is available and the relief of the ground. Oblique photographs of areas of high relief can only be successfully plotted if very small sections of the photograph are treated at one time; the method may then become tedious and inefficient. Photographs taken with distortion-free cameras over areas of low relief can be plotted quite accurately. Stereoscopic instruments help to reduce the problems caused by relief.

Archaeologists make extensive use of oblique photographs, often taken with non-metric cameras. The Royal Commission on Historical Monuments (England) has a large flying programme to cover ancient sites marked only by crop marks or similar indicators which often show up on oblique photographs (Hampton 1977). The detail from the photographs is transferred to Ordnance Survey maps using the Stereo Facet Plotter.

NUMERICAL TECHNIQUES

A second method of handling unconventional photography involves numerical techniques. The co-ordinates of an image on a photograph can be accurately measured on a comparator; either a single photograph or a pair of photographs can be measured. The image co-ordinates can be transformed using a suitable mathematical model determined from information about the camera found by calibration and ground control points. These methods can be very accurate and have been applied to a number of problems in many different fields. A specialist knowledge of photogrammetry is required and usually specially prepared computer programs are needed. Some examples of this type of application are for traffic studies; Garner and Heptinstall (1974) have described how the movement of traffic is measured and then transferred to a map; numerical techniques have been used for underwater photogrammetry, and, at the Grassland Research Institute, stereoscopic photographs have been used for the measurement of the growth of grass. This type of photography has been obtained from the ground, from kites, balloons, model aircraft and helicopters (Georgopoulos 1981). Automated methods can be applied to this type of processing. In Germany, Scollar (1979) has applied such methods to archaeological work; if points on a photograph are digitized and at least 4 control points are available, then a transformation can be computed and all the digitized points transformed can be plotted on an automatic drawing table. Scollar has gone one stage further and has made a digital record of the whole photograph by recording the densities and then transforming and reprinting the whole image. This is obviously an expensive and specialized technique, but equipment is now available to make large scale transformation of detail points accessible to a much wider user community.

Simple digitizing instruments can be connected to a computer and a plotting table to carry out transformations and plot the results. The Zeiss Stereocord G2 is one example of such an instrument which has been available for about 5 years now. Work done at University College London (Gibson 1977) has shown the potential of this type of equipment. More recently, other instruments have been developed and some examples are listed in Table 2. The cost and available software vary with the different instruments but computers and software can be selected according to requirements.

ANALYTICAL PLOTTING INSTRUMENTS

A more rigorous and convenient development than the simple digitizing and plotting instruments described above is the analytical plotter. This instrument can be operated in exactly the same way as an analogue plotting instrument, but what goes on inside is computer-controlled so that almost any type of photography can be handled and graphical or digital data can be produced in whatever

TABLE 2   Computer-assisted simple instruments for digitizing and numerical
plotting from photographs

Manufacturer	Model	Description
Officine Galileo, Florence, Italy	Digicart	Optical mechanical unit and computer which allows accurate reading and transformation of co-ordinates. Computer controlled removal of y-parallax.
OMI Rome, Italy	Automated Stereo Facet Plotter	Computer controlled version of Stereo Facet Plotter which gives automatic removal of x and y parallax over an area
Surveying & Scientific Instruments Ltd England		A range of digitizing, display and interfacing equipment is available so that a computer can give co-ordinates in real time
Carl Zeiss Oberkochen, W Germany	Stereocord G2	A parallax bar type device which is interfaced to a computer to correct image co-ordinates and compute heights

form is required. Such an instrument is therefore ideal for plotting from unconventional photographs.

The principle of the analytical plotter is described elsewhere (Dowman
1977) but an outline can be seen in Figure 2.

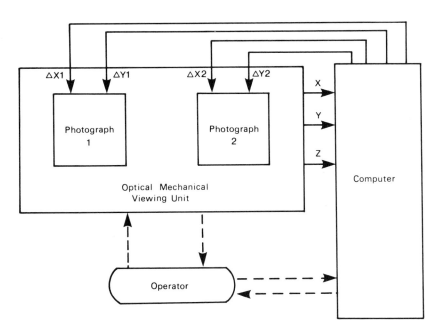

Figure 2   The principle of the analytical plotter

The operator inputs a set of ground co-ordinates by using the hand wheels and the foot wheel; the computer calculates the image co-ordinates relating to that ground position and drives the measuring marks to those positions on each photograph; this operation is carried out about 50 times each second. The measuring marks move as the operator moves the hand wheels and so the instrument appears to function in exactly the same way as a conventional analogue instrument. In order to determine the correct position of the image point, that is to create a model free of y-parallax and in correct absolute orientation, the position and attitude of each photograph at the time of exposure are needed. These are found during the setting up procedure and information is required about the camera, including distortion parameters and ground control. Because a computer is driving the photographs instead of a mechanical link, the relationship between image and model does not have to be linear but can take any suitable form to correct for lens distortion or other geometrical situations. Many analytical plotters incorporate optics which allow for the correction of scale changes and image rotation so that the operator can obtain comfortable stereoscopic viewing of photographs with different scales or large tilts. A plotting table can be connected to the computer to allow line drawings or profiles to be produced.

The advantages of the analytical plotter can be summarized as follows:

- there is no restriction on the tilt of the photographs except to give comfortable stereoscopic viewing with large tilts;

- there is no restriction on principal distance;

- the computer can correct any known distortion;

- the computer can carry out relative and absolute orientation when points are not in the standard positions;

- operating procedures are similar to analogue plotting instruments;

- plots can be produced or data stored in digital form;

- it allows rapid orientation and resetting of models;

- the computer can be used to drive and control movement in the model, for example to constrain movement along a particular line or in a set pattern.

Analytical plotters have become more widespread during the last 5 years and there are now several well proven and tested models and several more which have considerable potential. The instruments now available are listed in Table 3. The main use has been aerial triangulation in production organizations and non-topographical applications in universities and research establishments. Some of the non-topographical applications are:

- plotting contours of the human body;

- underwater photogrammetry;

- definition of flood plains;

- plotting architectural features;

- measuring structures in civil engineering;

- mapping from space imagery.

Analytical plotters vary in price from £50,000 to £150,000; this is not expensive by today's standards if the instrument is to be fully used; the problem is that many organizations would not have sufficient work to justify the cost. A single instrument could support the requirements of many small users. At present there is no analytical plotter in the United Kingdom available for civilian use, but the Department of Photogrammetry and Surveying at University College London has one on order* and it is hoped that, besides using it for teaching and research, outside bodies will make use of the facility and that, with the aid of money earned in that way, an efficient cost effective service unit can be established. The analytical plotter can provide a powerful and flexible tool for research and production and can extend the range of uses of unconventional photography.

TABLE 3   Analytical plotters currently available

Manufacturer	Model	Description	Approx cost excl. table £
Autometrics Inc, Virginia, USA	APPS IV	A microprocessor controlled instrument with limited power and accuracy	52,000
Canadian Marconi Co, Montreal, Canada	Anaplot II	A very sophisticated instrument with high accuracy and powerful computer	125,000
Helava Associates Inc, Michigan, USA	US-2	Advanced microprocessor control, high accuracy, standard host computer	55,000
Keuffel & Esser Co, Texas, USA	DSC-3/80	Optical mechanical unit interfaced to host computer	80,000
Kern & Co Ltd, Switzerland	DSR1	Advanced microprocessor control, high accuracy and standard host computer	45,000
Matra, Paris, France	Traster	Integral design incorporating computer and table with polaroid viewing screen	100,000 (includes table)
Officine Galileo, Florence, Italy	DS Digital Stereo-cartograph	Optical mechanical unit interfaced with host computer. Design imposes limitations on performance	50,000
OMI, Rome, Italy	APC-4	Long established range using optical mechanical unit interfaced with host computer	67,000
QASCO, Australia	SD-4	Basic instrument of novel design	12,500
Systemhouse Ltd, Ottawa, Canada	Autoplot	Optical mechanical unit interfaced with host computer	42,000
Wild Heerbrugg, Switzerland	AC 1	Well designed system with high accuracy and stand alone computer	111,000
Carl Zeiss, Oberkochen, W Germany	Planicomp	Well proven high accuracy system and good software	100,000

*Delivered and operating as at October 1982

CONCLUSIONS

If ecologists or others not familiar with photogrammetric techniques wish to use photographs for measuring or mapping, the best advice is to seek help from a photogrammetrist. However, some basic guidelines summarize the contents of this paper. First, always use the best camera that is available; if this is a non-metric camera, take steps to calibrate it, seeking help if necessary. Second, decide how the data will be plotted before taking the photographs and include appropriate ground control on the picture. Third, avoid oblique photographs if possible, as these contain the most errors and are the most difficult to deal with. If these basic rules are followed, and high accuracy is not required, then excellent results can be obtained at low cost.

REFERENCES

DOWMAN, I.J. 1977. Developments in on line techniques for photogrammetry and digital mapping. *Photogramm. Rec.*, 9(49), 41-54.

GARNER, J.B. & HEPTINSTALL, S.M. 1974. Semi automated transformation techniques for single aerial photographs. *Photogramm. Rec.*, 8(44), 222-228.

GEORGOPOULOS, A. 1981. *Low altitude non-metric photography in surveying*. Ph.D. thesis, University of London.

GIBSON, R.J. 1977. *The application of the Zeiss Stereocord G2 to topographic mapping*. M.Sc. thesis, University of London.

HAMPTON, J.M. 1977. Aerial reconnaissance for archaeology: uses of photographic evidence. *Photogramm. Rec.*, 9(50), 265-272.

SCOLLAR, I. 1979. Computer production of orthophotographs from single oblique images or from rotating mirror scanners. *Aerial Archaeol.*, 4(2), 17-27.

PROBLEMS IN THE REMOTE SENSING OF VEGETATION CANOPIES FOR BIOMASS ESTIMATION

P J CURRAN
Department of Geography, University of Sheffield, Sheffield

ABSTRACT

Ground based radiometry, aerial photography and satellite imagery can be used to estimate the Leaf Area Index (LAI), and thereby the green biomass of semi-natural vegetation, as the multispectral radiance of a vegetation canopy is strongly correlated to LAI. However, various factors which decrease the degree of correlation between the multispectral radiance of a vegetation canopy and its LAI require careful consideration if the biomass is to be accurately estimated and mapped.

INTRODUCTION

There is a relationship between the remotely sensed multispectral radiance of a vegetation canopy and the biomass of that canopy, which may be used to estimate vegetation biomass. The use of this method to estimate, map and monitor vegetation biomass has proven applications in agriculture and has potential applications for ecology and resource management. This paper will review the nature of the relationship between remotely sensed multispectral radiance and canopy biomass and will consider the theoretical and practical problems associated with the use of this method for biomass estimation.

THE REFLECTANCE OF RADIATION FROM A VEGETATION CANOPY

The earth's surface cover receives both direct and indirect solar irradiance, which is radiation incident on the surface of interest in Wm^{-2}; some of this is reflected, some is absorbed and some is transmitted. The ability of different surfaces to reflect, absorb and transmit this radiation varies considerably, thus presenting a method of identifying and extracting information about these surfaces. The radiation reflected by these surfaces, termed the radiant exitance in Wm^{-2}, is dependent upon the variable solar irradiance and is usually expressed in unitless reflectance values (Formula 1). This particular measurement of reflectance is termed hemispherical reflectance as it has no angular dependence, referring to irradiance and radiant exitance in all possible directions within a hemisphere.

$$\text{hemispherical reflectance} = \frac{\text{radiant exitance}}{\text{irradiance}} \qquad (1)$$

Studies of leaf reflectance have demonstrated that the hemispherical reflectance of light in the chlorophyll absorption bands, within the blue and red regions of the electromagnetic spectrum, is causally and negatively related to the amount of chlorophyll within the leaves (Whittingham 1974); and the hemispherical reflectance of near infrared radiation is causally and positively related to the degree of scattering that occurs as a direct consequence of discontinuities in the refractive indices within the leaf (Gausman 1974).

In remote sensing studies, the bidirectional reflectance (BDR) of a non-Lambertian vegetation canopy is measured. Non-Lambertian refers to a non-ideal imperfectly diffusing surface that does not reflect energy equally in all directions (Breece & Holmes 1971) and BDR refers to the ratio of the radiance of a target, under specified angular conditions of irradiance and viewing, to the radiance of a Lambertian reflector placed within the scene (Silva 1978).

The hemispherical reflectance of an individual leaf is insufficient to describe the remotely sensed BDR of a vegetation canopy (Simonett 1976; Leamer *et al.* 1978; Daughtry *et al.* 1980), because a vegetation canopy is not a large leaf but a mosaic of leaves, other plant structures, background and shadow. The BDR of the canopy is therefore primarily related to the area of the leaves recorded by the Leaf Area Index (LAI) (Leamer & Rosenberg 1975; Rao *et al.* 1979), rather than the hemispherical reflectance of the component leaves (Colwell 1974b). However, simple grass canopies with a high LAI have reflectance properties similar to those of a leaf, with a positive relationship between near infrared BDR and LAI and a negative relationship between red BDR and LAI (Tucker & Maxwell 1976).

THE RELATIONSHIP BETWEEN REMOTELY SENSED BDR AND LAI

The relationship between a ratio of remotely sensed red and near infrared BDR and LAI is curvilinear reaching an asymptote when the soil is completely covered by vegetation (Tucker 1977). However, for some sites, at times other than high summer, the sensed range of vegetation LAI is from 0 to 3 and, over this range, the relationship between both red and near infrared BDR and LAI can often be considered linear (see Figure 5).

Ratioing or differencing spectral data

In order to express the spectral data in values that relate to plant canopy characteristics, it is usual to use a spectral vegetation index (obtained by ratioing, differencing or otherwise transforming the spectral data (Jackson *et al.* 1980)).

Vegetation has a characteristically high BDR difference between regions of strong absorption in red wavebands, and regions of strong reflectance in near infrared wavebands. Variations between the BDR of different wavebands will provide a better estimate of LAI than one band alone and are, within certain limits, independent of varying solar irradiance and most soil types. This idea has been the basis of several waveband to waveband ratios (Table 1). The most popular BDR ratio is the vegetation index of normalized difference (Table 1) which offers simplicity, a high degree of standardization, and makes no assumptions as to the distribution of the data.

Transforming spectral data

There is a linear relationship between remotely sensed red and near infrared BDR for a range of soils or substrates (Figure 1), because light soils have both a high red and near infrared BDR and dark soils have both a low red and near infrared BDR (Curran *et al.* 1981). If vegetation grows on 2 bare soil sites A and B (see Figure 1), then at both sites the red BDR will probably decrease and the near infrared BDR will probably increase. This will result in the movement of the BDR co-ordinates for sites A_0 and B_0 to co-ordinates A_1 and B_1. The distances A_0 to A_1 and B_0 to B_1, are directly correlated to the LAI of the canopies at the 2 sites, and can be calculated from BDR data using the perpendicular vegetation index of Richardson and Wiegand (1977), in Table 1. If more than 2 wavebands are available, then further transforms are possible. For example, Kauth and Thomas (1976) use all of the 4 wavebands recorded by the Landsat satellite to construct 4 indices, of which the green vegetation index (Table 1) is similar to the perpendicular vegetation index and is directly correlated with LAI. Though more complicated than the indices based on ratioing or differencing, the transforms have the advantage of being independent of soil background and can therefore be used to compare the BDR of vegetation canopies over a wide area (Jackson *et al.* 1980). For example, American researchers have employed this so called 'signature extension' (Malila *et al.* 1980) to use the relationships derived in America, between a BDR transform, LAI and crop yield, to analyse Landsat data collected over Russia and China (MacDonald 1979).

TABLE 1   Seven of the more commonly used BDR ratios, where G = green, R = red and IR = near infrared

Name	Ratio	Examples
Simple subtraction	$IR-R$	Pearson *et al.* 1976
Simple division	$\dfrac{IR}{R}$	Curran & Milton 1983
Complex division	$\dfrac{IR}{R + \text{other wavebands}}$	Curran 1980b
Simple multiratio (vegetation index of normalized difference)	$\dfrac{IR - R}{IR + R}$	Curran 1982
Complex multiratio (transformed vegetation index or normalized difference)	$\sqrt{\dfrac{IR - R}{IR + R} + 0.5}$	Rouse *et al.* 1973
Perpendicular vegetation index (vegetation directional reflectance departure from soil background)	$\sqrt{(R_{soil} - R_{veg})^2 + (IR_{soil} - IR_{veg})^2}$	Richardson & Wiegand 1977
Green vegetation index (as above for use with Landsat satellite wavebands)	$-0.29(G) - 0.56(R) + 0.60(IR) + 0.49(IR)$	Kauth & Thomas 1976

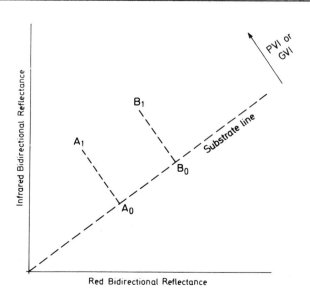

Figure 1   The co-ordinates of a red to infrared BDR plot for sites A and B, where A_0 and B_0 are bare soil and A_1 and B_1 are vegetation covered. The vegetation indices that can be used to record the spectral change from A_0 and B_0 to A_1 and B_1 are the perpendicular vegetation index or the green vegetation index (Table 1)

THE RELATIONSHIP BETWEEN REMOTELY SENSED RED AND NEAR INFRARED BDR AND VEGETATION BIOMASS

The degree of correlation between BDR and biomass is dependent upon the relationship between BDR and LAI, and the relationship between LAI and biomass. The only instances when BDR can be directly related to biomass are either when biomass changes independently of LAI, for example leaf thickening at times of high LAI, or, more commonly, when biomass is linearly related to LAI. This is so for non-woody monocotyledons of low biomass (eg grasses), where leaves may account for a constant and high proportion of the total biomass (Filzer 1951) and the relationship between BDR and LAI has the same form as the relationship between BDR and biomass (Figure 2a).

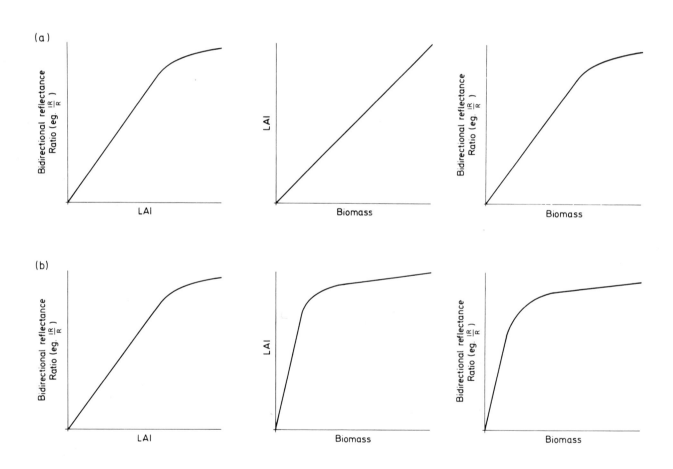

Figure 2   *The theoretical relationship between BDR, LAI and biomass for (a) a grass and (b) a tree canopy. Note that while grass canopy biomass can be used as a surrogate for LAI this is not so for the tree canopy*

For species with a high biomass, where either the proportion of leaves to total biomass is not constant (eg maize) or the leaves do not account for the majority of the biomass (eg shrubs), there will be a low degree of correlation between LAI and biomass and therefore a low degree of correlation between BDR and biomass (Figure 2b). In practice, the BDR for the majority of high biomass or woody species is not related to biomass over the full range found in the field, but is positively related at lower biomass (Figure 2b).

Before BDR can be used to estimate the biomass of a high biomass or woody species, the range over which BDR is significantly related to biomass must be determined. A Natural Environment Research Council funded pilot study was undertaken to determine the relationships between BDR recorded photographically, LAI and biomass for ling heather, *Calluna vulgaris*, on Snelsmore Common, a Site of Special Scientific Interest, in Berkshire, England. The relationship was linear, as the LAI was low and the reflectance asymptote was not reached (Figure 3). The relationship between biomass and both LAI and BDR (Table 2) was a function of the canopy morphology of *Calluna* (Gimingham 1972). For the growing (building), low biomass, sites there was a positive relationship between biomass and both LAI and BDR (Figure 4a and b); for the mature, medium biomass, sites the canopy was stable and there was no relationship between increasing biomass and higher values of either LAI or BDR; and for the early degenerate, high biomass, sites where the canopy was starting to open, there was a negative relationship between biomass and both LAI and BDR (Table 2, and Figure 4a and b). This pilot study has led to the use of BDR to monitor the early development of low biomass heather, following its damage by fire.

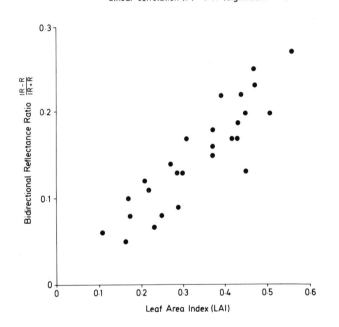

Linear correlation (r) = 0·89 (significant 1%)

Figure 3   The linear relationship between BDR, recorded photographically, and the LAI of Calluna

TABLE 2   Summary of the canopy development stages, biomass, LAI and BDR ratio for *Calluna vulgaris*

Stage of development	Canopy form	Biomass g/m^2	LAI and BDR ratio
Building	Rapidly growing immature canopy	<80	Low
Mature	Stable canopy at maximum height	80-180	High
Early degenerate	Central frame branches spreading apart exposing soil	>180	Medium

There is undoubtedly a useful relationship between multispectral reflectance and LAI for all green vegetation and a relationship between multispectral reflectance and biomass for some green vegetation; however, the strengths of these relationships show considerable variation with the environment. For example, with no change in the hemispherical reflectance of the individual leaves, the BDR of vegetation could vary appreciably due to the effect of the soil background, the presence of senescent vegetation, the scene and sensor geometry, and phenological and episodic canopy changes.

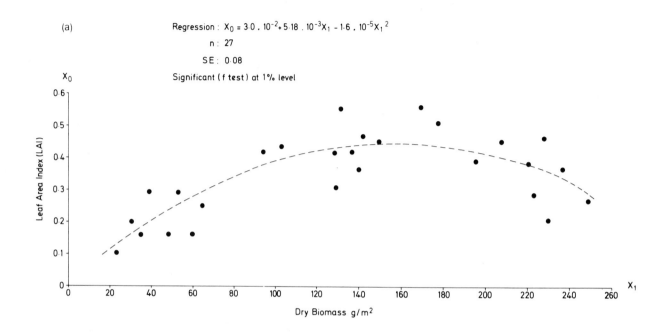

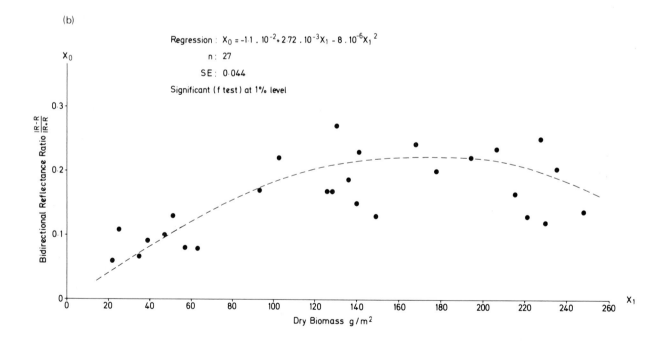

Figure 4   The polynomial relationship between (a) LAI and (b) BDR recorded photographically, and the dry biomass of Calluna, *where SE represents the standard error of the estimate*

PROBLEM 1 THE SOIL BACKGROUND

The BDR of the soil has a considerable effect on the remotely sensed BDR
of the canopy (Vinogradov 1969; Colwell 1974b; Berry *et al.* 1976; Idso *et al.*
1977). This is summarized in Figure 5, in which simulated green, red and near
infrared BDR are plotted against LAI. The soil/waveband combinations that are
unsuitable for remote sensing of vegetation can be identified; for example, on
dark soils, with low red BDR, there is little change in the red BDR with
increased LAI. On a light soil, with high BDR, the relationship between near
infrared BDR and LAI is weaker than on a dark soil with low BDR. These effects
of soil reflectance are illustrated by examples from the Somerset Levels and
Snelsmore Common in England, and the Kebili area of southern Tunisia.

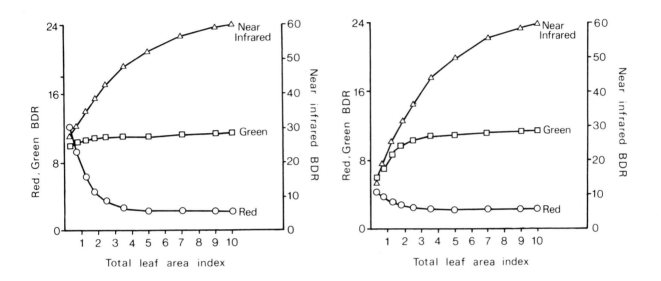

Figure 5   *The BDR of simulated vegetation canopies on a light soil (left) and
            a dark soil (right) in green, red and near infrared wavebands. Re-
            drawn from Colwell (1974b) and printed with the permission of the
            author*

Somerset levels, England

The Somerset Levels are an area of peatland used for the grazing of dairy
cattle (Curran 1979). Landsat 2 images of this area for 21 May 1977 are shown
in Plate 2. In the red waveband, the bare peat soil resulting from peat
extraction has a radiance similar to that of the surrounding vegetation and
the bare peat/vegetation boundary is not visible. In the near infrared waveband,
the radiance from the pasture is much greater than the radiance from the bare
peat; the bare peat/vegetation boundary is visible and any increase in vegetation biomass would also be visible. Therefore, on very dark soils, near infrared wavelengths will often be of greater value than red wavelengths for the
estimation of vegetation biomass.

Snelsmore Common, Berkshire, England

It has been shown that the cover of the heather at Snelsmore Common is
positively related to the remotely sensed near infrared BDR. However, the
actual values of near infrared BDR varied with the darkness of the soil (Figure
6). At any given cover value, wet soil decreased the near infrared BDR of the
canopy and dry soil increased it. As both red and near infrared wavebands are

Plate 2 *The Somerset levels, England, recorded by the satellite Landsat-2 on 27 May 1977. Both of the images are digitally enlarged to equal the map scale and represent 1/250th of a full Landsat scene. The upper image is recorded in an infrared (0.8-1.1 μm) waveband and the lower image is recorded in a red (0.6-0.7 μm) waveband*

similarly affected by a change in soil moisture content, it is customary to use a ratio of both red and near infrared BDR when estimating vegetation biomass (Table 1).

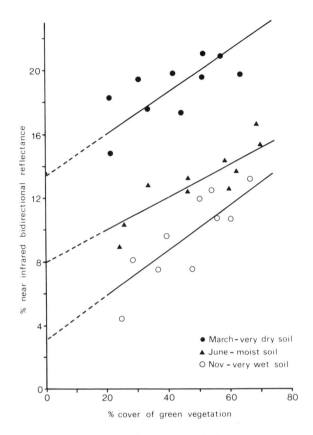

Figure 6   Ground based measurement of % near infrared BDR, plotted against the % cover of green vegetation at Snelsmore Common on 3 dates

Kebili area, southern Tunisia

In many arid and semi-arid regions of the world, the near infrared BDR can be higher from the soil than from the vegetation. This was the case in southern Tunisia (Figure 7) where the remotely sensed near infrared BDR from a salt crusted, silty, sand was so great that there was a negative relationship between near infrared BDR and the cover of the halophyte *Halocnemum strobilaceum*. Therefore, on these very light soils, red wavelengths will often be of equal value for the estimation of vegetation biomass.

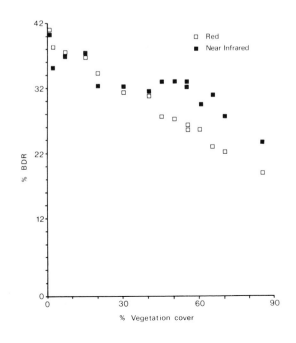

Figure 7   The relationship between % BDR recorded using a radiometer from head height and % vegetation cover for 15 sites in southern Tunisia. The vegetation is the halophyte Halocnemum strobilaceum *and the soil is a highly reflective salt crusted silty sand*

PROBLEM 2   SENESCENT VEGETATION

As vegetation dies, the near infrared leaf reflectance does not significantly decrease (Wooley 1971; Sinclair *et al.* 1973), although some argue otherwise (Milton 1981). The breakdown of plant pigments causes a rise in blue and red leaf reflectance (Sanger 1971). This results in a positive relationship between remotely sensed BDR, at each wavelength, and LAI (Tucker 1978). In semi-natural vegetation, senescence is a problem; a stand with an equal amount of live and dead components will have a positive relationship between near infrared BDR and LAI and probably no relationship between visible BDR and LAI. For many semi-natural sites in autumn, only near infrared BDR can be used to record LAI unless the proportion of dead vegetation within the canopy is known (Colwell 1974b; Curran 1981b).

PROBLEM 3   SCENE AND SENSOR GEOMETRY

The elevation and azimuth of the sensor and the sun, and the topography of the ground have a considerable effect on the remotely sensed BDR of a vegetation canopy.

Solar elevation

Two interrelated factors contribute to the effect of solar elevation on the BDR of a vegetation canopy: first, the degree to which solar radiation can penetrate the canopy; secondly, the amount of canopy shadow (Kimes *et al.* 1979).

Canopy penetration

When the sun is high in the sky, radiation is only transmitted through a few leaves before being reflected from the soil. At high solar elevation, radiation can penetrate deep into the canopy and reflectance is low. When the sun is low in the sky, the radiation is transmitted through many more leaves and barely reaches the soil. As a result, reflectance will be high (Ahmad & Lockwood 1979). This relationship is illustrated in Figure 8.

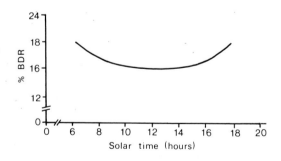

Figure 8   Calculated reflectance of a corn crop as a function of time on a clear day. (modified from Idso and de Witt (1970) and printed with the permission of the publisher)

Shadow

The effect of decreased BDR at high solar elevations is modified by shadow which tends to decrease the early morning and late evening BDR. This is most noticeable in wavebands where leaf transmittance is low and the shadow is dark, namely in the visible region up to wavelengths of 0.7 μm. In the near infrared (0.7-1.1 μm) wavelengths, where leaf transmittance is higher, shadow has less effect (Milton 1981). As a result, the majority of canopies had a negative relationship between near infrared reflectance and solar elevation and little or no relationship between visible reflectance and solar elevation (Figure 9) (Duggin 1977; Bauer *et al.* 1980).

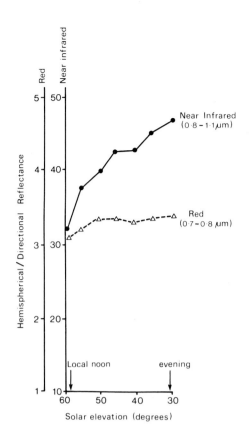

Figure 9   Hemispherical/directional reflect-ance (ratio of directional radiance to total irradiance) of a wheat canopy measured in red and near red infrared wavebands. Recorded from local (solar) noon until early evening (Modified from Duggin (1977) and printed with the permission of the publishers)

The effect of solar elevation is often not so pronounced under overcast conditions, as, when the sun is low in the sky, diffuse skylight will enable a greater proportion of the incoming radiation to penetrate the vegetation vertically. In fact, the reflectance properties of several canopies have been noted, by the author and others (Stewart 1971), to have very little variation with changing solar elevation under cloudy skies.

Sensor elevation

The angular elevation of the sensor determines the amount of soil and shadow seen, for, as the elevation moves from the vertical, the area of soil and shadow seen by the sensor decreases but the area of vegetation seen increases (Suits 1972a; Bauer *et al*. 1980). Therefore, a move from the vertical has a similar effect on the BDR as increasing vegetation cover.

The effect of solar elevation has been shown to be of particular importance for a sensor elevation within a few degrees of vertical. In Figure 10, a canopy

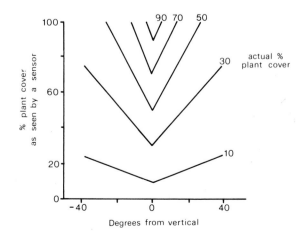

Figure 10   Fraction of a plant cover as a function of degrees from nadir for 5 values of actual plant cover with a height width ratio of 2. (Modified from Jackson et al. (1979) and printed with the permiss-ion of the publishers)

with a 90% cover, for example, located only 3.5° from the vertical (56 km) from the centre of a Landsat frame would appear to have a 100% cover. In Figure 11, the red and near infrared BDR of an 80% cover of the grasses *Lolium perenne* and *Poa* spp., recorded at a solar angle of 31° and an altitude of 10 m, are plotted against sensor elevation. A move of only 10° from the vertical increases the difference in BDR between the red and near infrared wavebands from 28% to 49% with no change in the LAI of the canopy. Not all vegetation is so sensitive to sensor elevation; for example, certain vegetation canopies with a high LAI (eg grassland), at high solar elevations, can appear to have a near Lambertian surface and, under these conditions, BDR can show little dependence upon sensor elevation (Egbert & Ulaby 1972). As this situation is relatively unusual and often unpredictable, it is customary to take measurements of BDR at a known sensor elevation (usually vertical) wherever possible. Future developments of satellite systems that use non-vertical sensors, for example the tentatively proposed NASA multispectral resource sampler (MRS) and the sensors on board the French SPOT satellite, necessitate increased research into the relationships between sensor elevation and BDR at given levels of biomass (Smith & Oliver 1974; Kriebel 1979; Smith *et al.* 1980b; Kirchner *et al.* 1981).

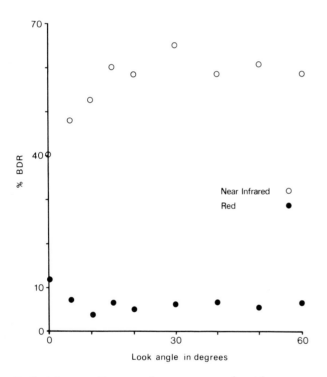

Figure 11   Red and near infrared BDR for a grass canopy with 80% ground cover, recorded using a radiometer at a number of look angles, from a height of 10 m

Relative solar and sensor azimuth

The BDR of a canopy is usually higher if the sensor is looking into, as opposed to away from, the sun, or away from the sun, as opposed to at right angles to the sun (Suits 1972b, Egbert & Ulaby 1972; Rao *et al.* 1979; Smith *et al.* 1980a). For the majority of remote sensing applications where the sensor look angle is near vertical, the effect of solar azimuth on BDR increases with a decrease in solar angle and an increase in vegetation canopy roughness. At high solar angles there is little shadow, and at low solar angles shadow is increased by an amount dependent upon the canopy roughness. To take an extreme example, when the sun is low in the sky and parallel to a row crop, the sensor will sense a greater proportion of soil reflectance and a lesser proportion of shadow reflectance than if the sun were at right angles to that row (Kauth & Thomas 1976; Jackson *et al.* 1979).

Canopy geometry

The geometry of a vegetation canopy will determine the amount of shadow seen by the sensor and will therefore influence the sensitivity of BDR measurements to angular variations in sun and sensor (Curran 1981b). For example, the BDR from a rough woodland canopy, unlike a smoother grassland canopy, is severely affected by the solar elevation.

Topography

The receipt of solar irradiance varies greatly with the elevation and azimuth of surface slopes. In Britain, for example, irradiance is high on south facing steep slopes and is low on north facing steep slopes. The effect of surface elevation and azimuth on BDR varies seasonally and diurnally with changes in the solar angle and azimuth. For example, Holben and Justice (1980) reported that one cover type at a solar elevation of 40° had a range of 52 Landsat pixel values in MSS 5 red wavelengths, as a result of variations in surface topography. Fortunately, in areas of undulating, as opposed to mountainous, terrain, visible radiation is similarly affected to near infrared radiation and therefore a waveband to waveband ratio can be used to suppress the effect of topography (Table 1).

PROBLEM 4 PHENOLOGY

The seasonal change in BDR, as recorded by aerial photography, is well documented (eg Steiner 1970). From quantitative studies it is known, for example, that for a non-deciduous (eg grassland) canopy the red BDR is maximized in the summer and minimized in the winter (Curran 1981a). These relationships have been presented in one of three ways: first, as plots of LAI (or biomass) and BDR against time (Rouse *et al*. 1973), second as BDR/LAI plot (Figure 2; Curran 1980a), and third, as a hysteresis loop of BDR (see Figure 12). Each hysteresis plot contains the expected seasonal pattern described above, with minor variations in this pattern for the vegetation of the nature reserve and maize crop, and major variations in this pattern for the wheat and rice crop. The wheat crop has lower than expected red BDR in the summer, due to its high productivity, and higher than expected near infrared BDR in the autumn, due to the presence of senescent stubble in the fields. Irrigation as well as vegetation LAI determines the BDR of the rice crop, as in the summer the wet soil background reduces the otherwise high near infrared BDR. These are examples where multitemporal, multispectral remote sensing of vegetation biomass is unlikely to be successful without adequate knowledge of the vegetation and sensor.

PROBLEM 5 EPISODIC EVENTS

Episodic events that significantly increase or decrease BDR while causing little or no change in LAI will decrease the degree of their correlation. For example, Suits (1972a), Colwell (1974a) and Collins (1978) reported that, for a canopy over a medium or dark toned soil, the change from a predominantly horizontal to a predominantly vertical leaf orientation (wilting) resulted in an increased red and decreased near infrared BDR, without any change in the LAI of the canopy. Similarly, changing cloud cover, dew formation on leaf surfaces, or leaves blowing in the wind can all affect the BDR.

In a small study area, it is possible to restrict the observation of BDR to times when short term canopy changes are minimal; but this is not possible for the satellite observation of large areas.

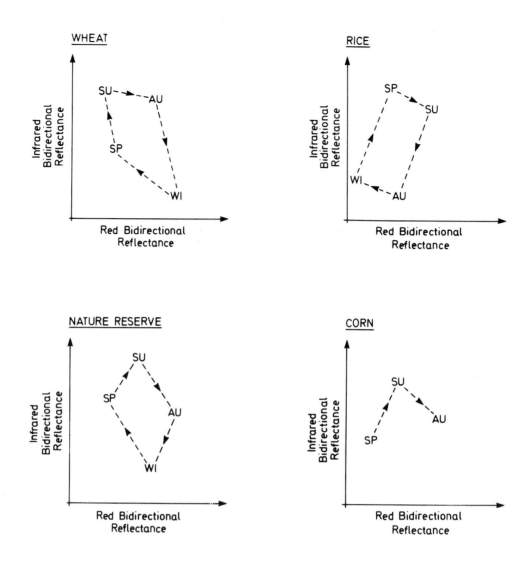

Figure 12   Four hysteresis loops for the seasonal development of vegetation:
wheat (Kauth & Thomas 1976), rice (Tanaka et al. 1977), nature
reserve (Curran 1980b) and maize (Tucker et al. 1979). Spring,
autumn, summer, winter are abbreviated as SP, AU, SU, WI respectively

CONCLUSIONS

The use of remotely sensed data to estimate biomass has attacted attention
not simply because the majority of remotely sensed scenes are in part vegetation
covered but because the spatial distribution of biomass has ecological and
economic importance. Research effort has been aimed at monitoring agricultural
biomass and more recently semi-natural biomass by multispectral means, in order to
determine the influence of a variety of environmental and also sensor effects.
Only when these effects are understood, at the scale of the leaf, canopy and
field, can there be accurate remote sensing of biomass and the application of
these techniques to ecological mapping and management.

REFERENCES

AHMAD, S.B. & LOCKWOOD, J.G. 1979. Albedo. *Prog. phys. Geogr.*, <u>3</u>, 500-543.
BAUER, M.E., BIEHL, L.L. & ROBINSON, B.F., eds. 1980. *Field research on the
spectral properties of crops and soils*. West Lafayette, Indiana: Purdue
University, Laboratory for the Application of Remote Sensing.

BERRY, J.K., SMITH, J.A. & RANSON, K.J. 1976. *Signature extension for spectral variation in soils. Volume IV: Final report, Earth Observations Division.* NAS 9-14467. Houston, Texas: NASA.

BREECE, H.T. & HOLMES, R.A. 1971. Bidirectional scattering characteristics of healthy green soybean and corn leaves *in vivo. Appl. Opt.,* 10, 119-127.

COLLINS, W. 1978. Remote sensing of crop type and maturity. *Photogramm. Eng. & Remote Sens.,* 44, 43-55.

COLWELL, J.E. 1974a. Vegetation canopy reflectance. *Remote Sens. Environ.,* 3, 175-183.

COLWELL, J.E. 1974b. Grass canopy bidirectional spectral reflectance. *Proc. int. Symp. Remote Sens. Environ., 9th, Ann Arbor, Michigan,* 1061-1085.

CURRAN, P.J. 1979. The peatlands of central Somerset and their utilisation. *Proc. Bristol Nat. Soc.,* 37, 85-89.

CURRAN, P.J. 1980a. Multispectral remote sensing of vegetation amount. *Prog. phys. Geogr.,* 4, 315-341.

CURRAN, P.J. 1980b. Multispectral photographic remote sensing of vegetation amount and productivity. *Proc. int. Symp. Remote Sens. Environ., 14th, Ann Arbor, Michigan,* 623-637.

CURRAN, P.J. 1981a. *Small format light aircraft photography.* (Geographical Papers). Reading: Reading University.

CURRAN, P.J. 1981b. Multispectral remote sensing of vegetation biomass and productivity. In: *Plants and the daylight spectrum,* edited by H. Smith, 65-69. London: Academic Press.

CURRAN, P.J. 1982. Multispectral photographic remote sensing of vegetation amount and productivity. *Photogramm. Eng. & Remote Sens.,* 48, 243-250.

CURRAN, P.J. & MILTON, E.J. 1983. The relationship between the chlorophyll concentration, LAI and bidirectional reflectance of a simple vegetation canopy. *Int. J. Remote Sens.,* 4, in press.

CURRAN, P.J., MUNDAY, T.J. & MILTON, E.J. 1981. A comparison between two photographic methods for the determination of relative bidirectional reflectance. *Int. J. Remote Sens.,* 2, 185-188.

DAUGHTRY, C.S.T., BAUER, M.E., CRECELIUS, D.W. & HIXSON, M.M. 1980. *Effects of management practices on reflectance of spring wheat canopies.* (LARS Technical Report no. SR-PO-00458, NAS 9-15466). West Lafayette, Indiana: Purdue University Laboratory for the Application of Remote Sensing.

DUGGIN, M.J. 1977. Likely effects of solar elevation on the quantification of changes in vegetation with maturity using sequential imagery. *Appl. Opt.,* 16, 521-533.

EGBERT, D.D. & ULABY, F.T. 1972. Effects of angles on reflectivity. *Photogramm. Eng.,* 38, 556-563.

FILZER, P. 1951. *Die naturlichen Grundlagen des Pflanzenertrages in Mitteleuropa.* Stuttgart: Swiezbart.

GAUSMAN, H.W. 1974. Leaf reflectance of near infrared. *Photogramm. Eng.,* 40, 183-191.

GIMINGHAM. C.H. 1972. *Ecology of heathlands.* London: Chapman & Hall.

HOLBEN, B.N. & JUSTICE, C.O. 1980. The topographic effect on spectral response from nadir pointing sensors. *Photogramm. Eng. & Remote Sens.,* 46, 1191-1200.

IDSO, S.B. & de WITT, C.T. 1970. Light relations in plant canopies. *Appl. Opt.,* 9, 177-184.

IDSO, S.B., REGINATO, R.J. & JACKSON, R.D. 1977. Albedo measurement for remote sensing of crop yields. *Nature, Lond.,* 266, 625-628.

JACKSON, R.D., PINTER, P.J., IDSO, S.B. & REGINATO, R.J. 1979. Wheat spectral reflectance. Interactions between crop configuration, sun elevation, and azimuth angle. *Appl. Opt.,* 18, 3730-3732.

JACKSON, R.D., PINTER, P.J., REGINATO, R.J. & IDSO, S.B. 1980. *Hand-held radiometry.* Phoenix, Arizona: SEA/AR Workshop on Hand-held Radiometry.

KAUTH, R.G. & THOMAS, G.S. 1976. The tasseled cap: a graphic description of the spectral-temporal development of agricultural crops as seen by Landsat. *Proc. Symp. Machine Processing of Remotely Sensed Data,* 6.23-7.2. (IEEE Cat. No. 76). West Lafayette, Indiana: Purdue University, Laboratory for the Application of Remote Sensing.

KIMES, D.S., SMITH, J.A. & RANSON, K.J. 1979. *Interpreting vegetation reflectance measurements as a function of solar zenith angle.* (Technical Memorandum 80320). Houston, Texas: NASA/GSFC.

KIRCHNER, J.A., SCHNECTZIER, C.C. & SMITH, J.A. 1981. Simulated directional radiances of vegetation from space platforms. *Int. J. Remote Sens.,* 2, 253-264.

KRIEBEL, K.T. 1979. Albedo of vegetated surfaces: its variability with differing irradiances. *Remote Sens. Environ.,* 8, 283-290.

LEAMER, R.W. & ROSENBERG, N.J. 1975. Modification of soybean canopy radiation balance. II. A quantitative and qualitative analysis of radiation reflected from a green soybean canopy. *Agron. J.,* 67, 301-306.

LEAMER, R.W., NORIEGA, J.A. & WIEGAND, C.L. 1978. Seasonal changes in reflectance of two wheat cultivars. *Agron. J.,* 70, 113-118.

MacDONALD, R.B. 1979. A technical description of the Large Area Crop Inventory Experiment, *Proc. Techn. Sess.,* vols 1 and 11. JSC 16015. Houston, Texas: NASA.

MALILA, W.A., LAMBECK, P.E., CRIST, E.P., JACKSON, R.J. & PINTER, P.J. 1980. Landsat features for agricultural applications. *Proc. int. Symp. Remote Sens. Environ., 14th, Ann Arbor, Michigan,* 793-803.

MILTON, E.J. 1981. Empirical studies of the reflectance of complex natural surfaces using the Milton multiband radiometer. *Int. Coll. Spectral Signatures of Objects in Remote Sensing, Avignon, France, 1981,* 173-181.

PEARSON, R.L., TUCKER, C.J. & MILLER, L.D. 1976. Spectral mapping of shortgrass prairie biomass. *Photogramm. Eng. & Remote Sens.,* 42, 317-323.

RAO, V.R., BRACH, E.J. & MACK, A.R. 1979. Bidirectional reflectance of crops and the soil contribution. *Remote Sens. Environ.,* 8, 115-125.

RICHARDSON, A.J. & WIEGAND, C.L. 1977. Distinguishing vegetation from soil background. *Photogramm. Eng. & Remote Sens.,* 43, 1541-1552.

ROUSE, J.W., HAAS, R.H., SCHELL, J.A. & DEERING, D.W. 1973. Monitoring vegetation systems in the Great Plains with ERTS. *Symp. Earth Resources Technology Satellite, 3rd,* 309-317. (NASA Sp-351(1)).

SANGER, J.E. 1971. Quantitative investigations of leaf pigment from their inception in buds through autumn colouration to decomposition in falling leaves. *Ecology,* 52, 1075-1089.

SILVA, L.F. 1978. Radiation and instrumentation in remote sensing. In: *Remote sensing: the quantitative approach,* edited by P.H. Swain and S.M. Davis, 121-135. New York: McGraw Hill.

SIMONETT, D.S. 1976. Remote sensing of cultivated and natural vegetation: crops and forest land. In: *Remote sensing of environment,* edited by J. Lintz and D.S. Simonett, 442-481. London: Addison-Wesley.

SINCLAIR, T.R., SCHREIBER, M.M. & HOFFER, R.M. 1973. Diffuse reflectance hypothesis for the pathway of solar radiation through leaves. *Agron. J.,* 65, 276-283.

SMITH, J.A. & OLIVER, R.E. 1974. Effects of changing canopy directional reflectance on feature selection. *Appl. Opt.,* 13, 1599-1604.

SMITH, J.A., RANSON, K.J. & KIRCHNER, J.A. 1980a. *Simulation analysis of bidirectional reflectance properties and their effects on scene radiance.* Silver Spring, Maryland: ORI Inc. Report to NASA.

SMITH, J.A., LIN, T.L. & RANSON, K.J. 1980b. The Lambertian assumption and Landsat data. *Photogramm. Eng. & Remote Sens.,* 46, 1183-1189.

STEWART, J.B. 1971. The albedo of a pine forest. *Q. Jl R. Met. Soc.,* 97, 561-564.

STEINER, D. 1970. Time dimension for crop surveys from space. *Photogramm. Eng.,* 36, 187-194.

SUITS, G.H. 1972a. The calculation of the directional reflectance of a vegetative canopy. *Remote Sens. Environ.,* 2, 117-125.

SUITS, G.H. 1972b. The cause of azimuthal variations in directional reflectance of vegetative canopies. *Remote Sens. Environ.,* 2, 175-182.

TANAKA, S., MURANDKA, Y., MIYAZAWA, H. & SUGA, Y. 1977. Multiseasonal data analysis and some extensions for environmental monitoring. *Proc. int. Symp. Remote Sens. Environ., 11th, Ann Arbor, Michigan,* 1-18.

TUCKER, C.J. 1977. Asymptotic nature of grass canopy spectral reflectance. *Appl. Opt.*, 16, 1151-1157.

TUCKER, C.J. 1978. Post-senescent grass canopy remote sensing. *Remote Sens. Environ.*, 7, 203-210.

TUCKER, C.J. & MAXWELL, E.L. 1976. Sensor design for monitoring vegetation canopies. *Photogramm. Eng. & Remote Sens.*, 42, 1399-1410.

TUCKER, C.J., ELGIN, J.H. & McMURTREY, J.E. 1979. Temporal spectral measurements of corn and soybean crops. *Photogramm. Eng. & Remote Sens.*, 45, 643-653.

VINOGRADOV, B.W. 1969. Remote sensing of the arid zone vegetation in the visible spectrum for studying productivity. *Proc. int. Symp. Remote Sens. Environ., 6th, Ann Arbor, Michigan,* 1237-1250.

WHITTINGHAM, C.P. 1974. *The mechanisms of photosynthesis*. London: Edward Arnold.

WOOLEY, J.T. 1971. Reflectance and transmittance of light by leaves. *Pl. Physiol. Lancaster,* 47, 656-662.

EFFECTS OF SPATIAL RESOLUTION ON THE CLASSIFICATION OF LAND COVER TYPE

J R G TOWNSHEND

Department of Geography, University of Reading, Whiteknights, Reading

ABSTRACT

The resolving power of sensors on board current and future Earth resources satellites is outlined in terms of the most commonly used measure, namely the instantaneous field of view. The potentially misleading character of this measure is described. Simulation experiments have shown that improvements in classification accuracy do not necessarily follow from finer spatial resolution, and indeed accuracies may well decline. The nature of the relationship between classification accuracy and resolution is shown to be a function of intra-unit variability as described by scene noise, inter-unit variability characterized by boundary density, and the relative location of classes within the feature space. Exploitation of the extra data provided by higher resolution sensors will have to rely on the use of spatial characteristics, including both textural and contextual measures.

RESOLVING POWER OF CURRENT AND FUTURE EARTH RESOURCES SATELLITES

Within the next 5 years, imagery from Earth resources satellites will have significantly better spatial resolving powers, compared with that generally available today (Jackson & Plevin this symposium). Currently, imagery suitable for Earth resources investigations is almost entirely from the Landsat Multispectral Scanner System (MSS) with a spatial resolution of 79 m, as defined by the instantaneous field of view (IFOV). The Thematic Mapper (TM) on board Landsat D will have a resolution approximately 3 times as good and the multispectral linear array on the French SPOT more than 4 times as good: in areal terms, these represent improvements by factors of 9 and more than 16 times respectively.

This paper discusses the benefits to be gained from such improvements in spatial resolution, and also the problems which need to be overcome if the imagery is to be used effectively. Before moving to a discussion of these matters it is important to define spatial resolution more precisely, and in particular to explain the meaning of IFOV, which is the measure of resolution most commonly quoted for Earth resources satellites.

Loosely, spatial resolution refers to the fineness of detail which is represented within an image. For most satellite sensors, we can quantify spatial resolution in terms of the IFOV, which is derived from the focal length of the sensor, height of the satellite above ground level and the size of the detector (Figure 1). Expressed as an angular measure or a ground distance, this might appear to be a totally satisfactory measure of spatial resolution. For various reasons, the IFOV can be quite misleading to the unwary. First, it does not always indicate the smallest object which can be detected. If they are very bright, small objects can affect the spectral response of a whole pixel. For example, a mirror only 300 mm across will completely saturate the received signal of the Landsat MSS for a whole pixel if pointed precisely to reflect sunlight at the satellite (Slater 1980). A more apposite example may be taken from the Advanced Very High Resolution Radiometer (AVHRR) on board the US National Oceanic and Atmospheric Administration's satellites NOAA 6 and 7. This sensor has a coarse resolution of 1.1 km, its imagery being used primarily for atmospheric and oceanographic applications. Channel 3 of this sensor responds to thermally emitted radiation and it has been found that a forest fire occupying only 2% of a pixel is sufficient completely to saturate the signal. Thus, relatively small forest fires in the western US have been detected before identification at ground level (S Schneider, NOAA/National Environment Satellite Service, personal communication, August 1981).

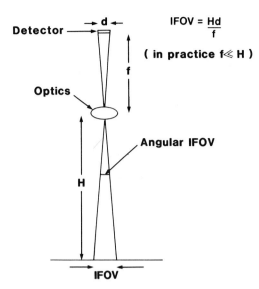

Figure 1   Definition of the geometric instantaneous field of view (IFOV)

Conversely, the IFOV does not indicate that all objects greater than its dimensions will necessarily be detected. Usually we find that areas of common cover types need to be between 2 and 3 times that of the pixel dimensions for them to be clearly detectable. Explanation for this can, in part, be found from a consideration of the noise present in a signal. Any signal will contain noise, that is random variations due to factors other than the target being imaged. Various types of noise are always present, including shot noise due to random fluctuations of photons striking the detector and Johnson noise caused by internal thermal effects. The atmosphere also introduces a noise-like phenomenon (Fraser 1974), as does quantization when we convert the analogue signal from the sensor into a digital signal suitable for computer-assisted analysis. All these effects will tend to reduce the contrast between objects, and thus small objects in particular may well be inseparable.

Also of significance are blurring effects caused by such factors as aberration in lenses, the motion of aircraft and mirrors within scanners. A blurring effect is also introduced by a lack of perfect registration between multispectral images.

For all these reasons it is unwise to assume that objects similar in size to the IFOV will be consistently detectable. One exception to this is where the object is very long relative to its width, such as a river or road; in this case the width may be similar or even smaller than the IFOV and still be consistently detectable.

Not surprisingly, various other measures of spatial resolution have been introduced which take account of some of the effects we have described (Townshend 1981a); unfortunately, such measures of spatial resolution are much less common than the IFOV. Hence we must rely on this measure, but at the same time we must be aware of its limitations. An alternative approach to the measurement of resolution is the estimation of the minimum area which can be classified accurately; this is discussed later.

CONSEQUENCES OF IMPROVING SPATIAL RESOLUTION

In order to assess the benefits to be gained from improving spatial resolution, several experiments have been performed using aircraft images. These are then progressively degraded to simulate images with coarser resolutions. Relatively little experimental work has been performed on the effects of spatial resolution on the visual interpretation of imagery. However, the results of Lauer and Thaman (1971) are probably indicative of the general trends, indicating, as they do, a monotonic increase in correct identification with finer spatial resolution. This expected result is so strongly shown because of the reliance of the human image interpreter on spatial features rather than simple tonal values. Visually, we can appreciate this point by examining Plate 3 which shows images of the same scene with various spatial resolutions. It is interesting to note that for this area the change from 10 m to 20 m is probably the most significant one in terms of visual interpretation. Note that the coarsest resolution depicted is approximately half that of the Landsat MSS.

Usually the human interpreter's requirements will be for imagery with the highest resolutions possible. Such an attitude may well be naive: the value of information extractable from imagery is often strongly determined by the type of image enhancement used (Townshend 1981b). If there is reliance on digital methods for such enhancement, the computing times involved will be strongly dependent on the amount of data present, and this will depend directly on spatial resolution.

Increasingly, information is extracted from images not by human interpreters but by computer-assisted classification techniques (Swain & Davis 1978; Townshend 1981b; Baker this symposium; Ritchie & Stove this symposium). Currently these tend to rely heavily on the digital values (in visual terms 'tones') of pixels and often do not rely on spatial information at all. The basic procedure normally adopted is to define a multidimensional feature space, where each axis represents values from each of the channels of the sensor. Using a subsample of the pixels, for which ground conditions are known, the feature space is partitioned into subspaces, each of which contains a single cover class so far as is possible. Assuming such a partitioning proves successful, then extrapolation to the remainder of the scene is performed, classifying the pixels according to decision rules representing the boundaries of the subspaces.

Scene noise

If, within an image, we restrict ourselves to those pixels which do not fall on the boundaries between cover types, we find that classification accuracy tends to worsen as we improve resolution (Thomson *et al.* 1974; Kan *et al.* 1975; Clark & Bryant 1977; Landgrebe *et al.* 1977). Examples of this phenomenon can be seen in Figure 2a.

This unexpected reduction in classification accuracy principally arises because cover types appear more and more heterogeneous as resolution improves (Figure 2b). For example, in an area of woodland, as resolution becomes finer, differences in canopy illumination become visible as do gaps in the canopy. Thus, the variability of the signal of a given category will increase and contrasts between cover types will be reduced. This effect is similar to that of noise described above and consequently has been termed *scene* noise (Wiersma & Landgrebe 1978). A simple measure of scene noise is the variance or standard deviation of the digital value. As shown by Figure 2, with the exception of water, there is a clear decline in scene noise as resolution improves. The standard deviation for water changes very little because the near infrared band absorbs almost all the received radiation and the variability recorded is almost entirely a function of other types of noise which are present.

(a)

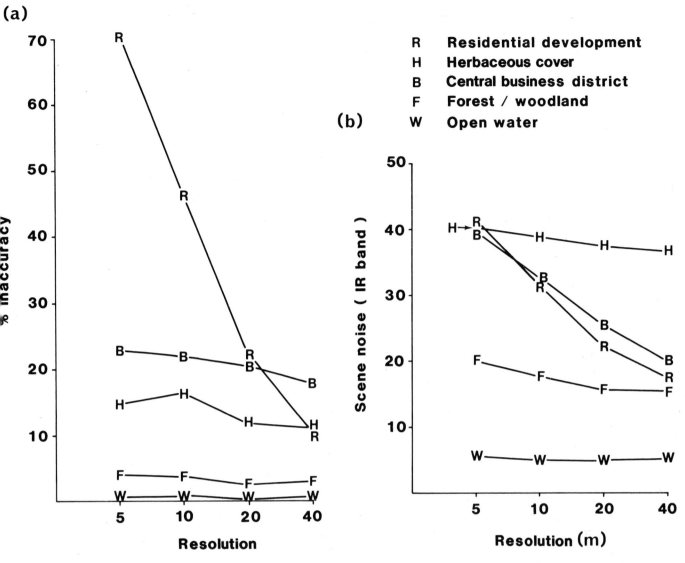

(b)

R **Residential development**
H **Herbaceous cover**
B **Central business district**
F **Forest / woodland**
W **Open water**

Figure 2   *Changing (a) classification accuracy (b) scene noise (as measured*
by standard deviation of spectral response), with coarsening
resolution (IFOV (m)). Depending on the category, scene noise
clearly can change at very different rates. Data derived from
progressively degraded aircraft images

Thus, as resolution becomes finer, the scene noise increases and hence
the volume of the feature space which is occupied by a particular category
expands, and overlap with other categories becomes more probable (Figure 3).
Consequently, classification accuracies are likely to decline with improving
resolution. As this example illustrates, the rate of change of classification
accuracy with resolution is not simply a function of the differing rates of
scene noise with resolution. The residential and business district categories
have similar high rates of change of scene noise (Plate 3), but accuracy of
classification of residential development increases much more rapidly with
finer spatial resolution. Reference to Figure 3 provides an explanation, where
the much more central location of the residential category within the feature
space is apparent, compared with the central business category. Thus, mis-
classifications are much more likely in the case of the former category. In
summary, the way in which changes of scene noise affect classification of any
one category is strongly affected by the relative positions of other categories
within the feature space.

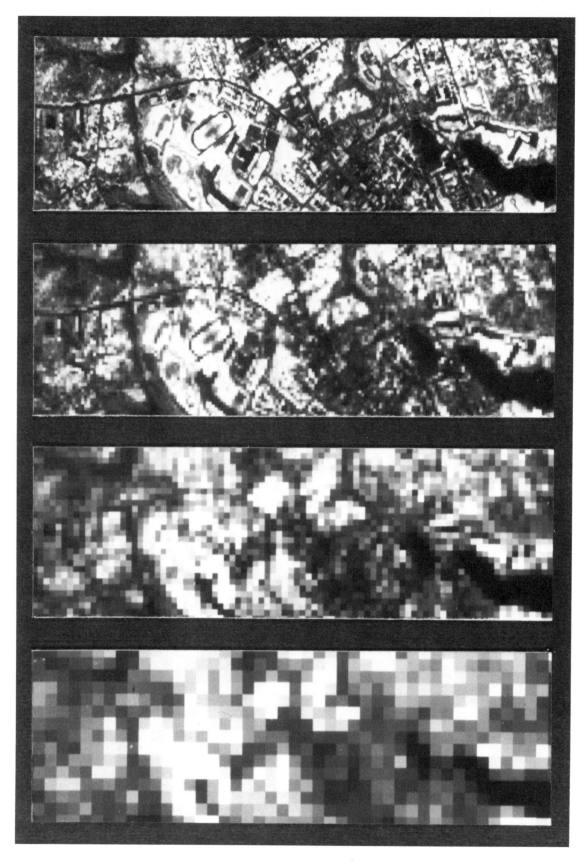

Plate 3   Effect of changing resolution on the appearance of a near infrared image near Annapolis, Maryland. Highest resolution image derived from a M²S multispectral scanner mounted in an aircraft flying at c. 2000 m, IFOV - 5 m: Image degraded to simulate sensor resolutions of 10 m, 20 m and 40 m

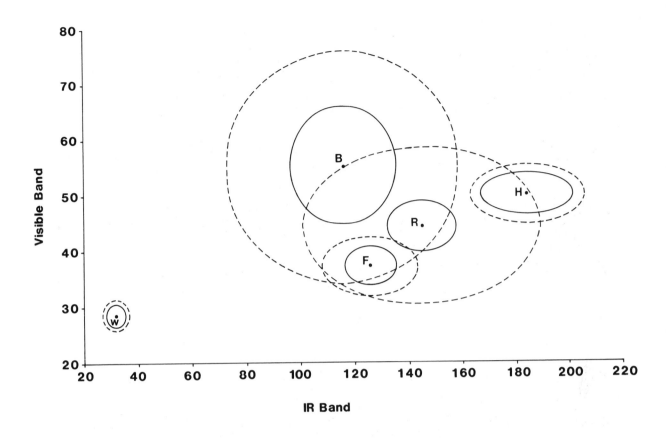

Figure 3   *Significance of position of land cover categories within a feature space on the way in which classification accuracy changes with resolution. The larger ellipses are at one standard deviation at 5 m resolution and the smaller ellipses are at one standard classification at 40 m resolution. Note the residential category surrounded by the other categories is the one showing the most marked improvement with coarsening resolution (see Plate 4)*

R — residential development; H — herbaceous cover; B — central business district; F — forest/woodland; W — open water

Resultant classified images of the Annapolis area are shown in Plate 4 for 4 different resolutions. Note that, in certain parts of the image, especially in the lowest part, there is relatively little change in the classified images with coarsening resolution. In other parts, major changes can be seen, notably in the central area where there is a considerable increase in the amount of residential development detected relative to the other classes as a result of declining scene noise with coarser resolution, as discussed above.

Boundary frequency effects

Our previous discussion has been concerned exclusively with pixels which do not fall across the boundaries between cover categories. If, however, we include these boundary pixels, then there will be a counteracting effect to that of scene noise: that is, as resolution becomes finer, classifications will tend to improve. This is because boundary pixels are inherently more likely to be misclassified. Not only may a mixed pixel be allocated to one or other of the classes on each side of the boundary, but it may even be assigned to a third com-

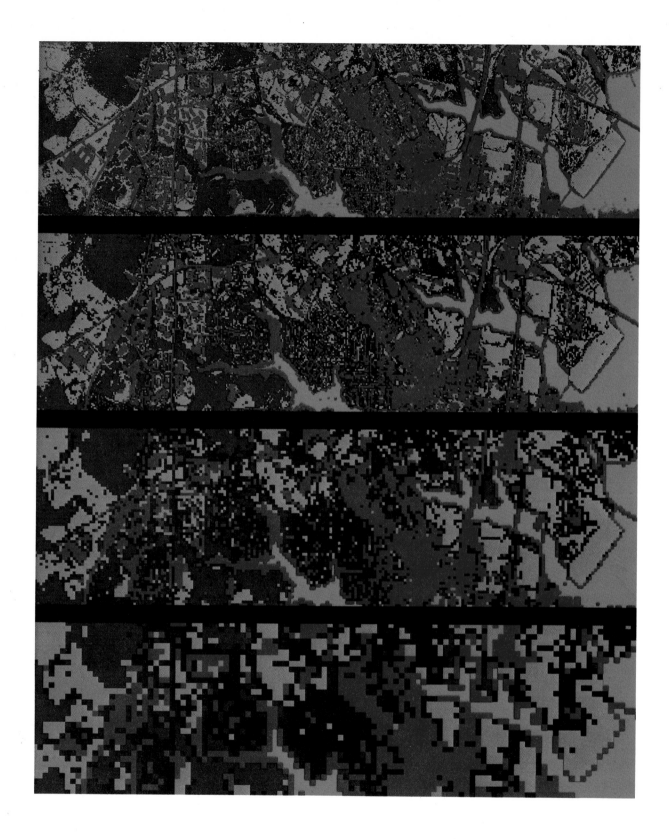

Plate 4   Changes in classification maps with coarsening resolution of imagery.
Classification was performed using a maximum likelihood classifier
with a 3 band image. Resolutions shown are 5 m, 10 m, 20 m and 40 m.
Colour key: red - central urban; dark green - residential development (low density); yellow - herbaceous cover; light green - woodland;
blue - open water. Figure 3 shows the raw data of part of this scene

pletely different category. Even if the latter does not occur, there is no guarantee that the boundary pixels will be proportionately correctly assigned to the 2 categories. Improved resolution inevitably leads to a decline in the proportion of boundary pixels within a scene, and hence classification accuracies will increase.

Given the inherent counteracting effects of boundary frequency and scene noise, the way in which classification accuracies will change with resolution is indeterminable without consideration of the spatial properties of the area of terrain being imaged. As Figure 4 shows, scene noise effects may dominate, or boundary effects may dominate, or there may be a balance between the two. In the latter case, we obtain the rather remarkable result that changing resolution over wide ranges may have relatively little effect on classification accuracy. Moreover, for any given scene we might expect that, if we start with very coarse resolutions and make them progressively finer, there will be an improvement in classification accuracy as the proportion of boundary pixels decline, they will level off as boundary effects and scene noise effects are balanced, and, as scene noise effects inevitably dominate, the accuracy will finally decline. Consequently, for classifiers dependent on values of individual pixels there will be an optimal band of resolutions above and below which classification accuracies will decline. Apart from the per-point classifiers described above, there are many others which use spatial information of various sorts, and these might well be especially useful when higher resolution imagery is used. Either textural or contextual classifiers may well prove of value. Textural classifiers use descriptions based on the spatial arrangement of a group of pixels. Contextual classifiers rely on information concerning the spatial relationships of an individual pixel with the remainder of the scene. For example, we might wish to modify the class of a pixel on the basis of the class of other surrounding pixels (Townshend & Justice 1981). Although classifiers relying on such spatial information should potentially be able to benefit from the extra spatial information contained within higher resolution imagery, this will only be gained at the expense of longer computing times.

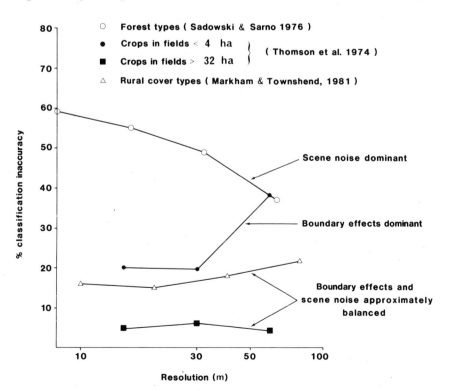

Figure 4   Changing classification accuracy with coarsening resolution showing interacting effects between scene noise and boundary frequency on classification accuracy

MINIMUM CLASSIFIABLE AREA

In the previous section, we assessed the significance of boundary pixels relative to the effects of internal variation within cover classes. It was noted that boundary pixels are inherently more difficult to classify than pure pixels. Consequently the smaller an areal unit, the less likelihood there is that it will be classified accurately. If we can estimate the minimum classifiable area, it should then be possible *a priori* to decide whether a given satellite system is suitable for a given task of ground cover discrimination, assuming we have an estimate of the size of the areal units on the ground.

Estimates of minimum classifiable areas have normally been based on regular agricultural fields, usually with the assumption for the sake of simplicity that pixel boundaries are parallel with the field sides. However, the conclusions are clearly broadly applicable to all types of areal units. The approach adopted by Shay *et al.* (1975) was based on a requirement to have at least 30 interior pixels per field. This had been determined from photo-interpretation requirements for accurate identification of fields. The number of interior pixels was expressed as follows:

$$nc-4\sqrt{nc}$$

where n is the size of the field and c is the number of resolution cells per unit area. If this expression equals 30, then nc the number of pixels in the field must be 61, and for a square field it will have dimensions of $\sqrt{61}$. In fact it appears from geometrical considerations that the expression should be $nc-4(\sqrt{nc}-1)$, therefore yielding a value of 56 rather than 61. Viglione *et al.* (1975) argued that at least half the pixels in a field should be field centre (non-boundary) pixels. Using data from Thomson *et al.* (1974), it was determined that, for typical fields of 4.05 ha, a 30 m resolution results in this criterion being fulfilled and hence 45 pixels is the estimated minimum area accurately classifiable. The formula proposed by Shay *et al.* (1975) is based on the assumption that pixels cover the field so as to maximize the proportion of boundary pixels. Simply by shifting the pixel boundaries relative to the margins of the field, a far smaller area of the field is covered by boundary pixels. The minimum value for the number of boundary pixels is then: $nc-2(\sqrt{nc}-1)$. In this case nc = 41, which represents the minimum field size required. Empirical evidence from the CITARS experiment suggested that consistently correct classifications could be achieved using Landsat MSS data for fields as small as 13.2 ha (Shay *et al.* 1975). As one Landsat MSS pixel is 0.44 ha, this yields a minimum size of 30 pixels. Finally, in a simulation experiment comparing the capabilities of the MSS with the TM, the assumption was made that the minimum classifiable area was 16 pixels (ie 4 x 4) but without any substantive evidence being presented to support it (General Electric 1975).

The resulting relationships between minimum classifiable area and the IFOV have been plotted on Figure 5. As can be seen, there is an almost fourfold variation in the estimate of minimum field size for any given IFOV though, if we exclude the lowest value of 16 pixels for which no substantive support was provided, the range is only twofold, and somewhat less if we exclude the highest value of 61 pixels which is apparently the result of a mathematical error.

In fact, it should not be expected that a single value of the minimum classifiable area for any given IFOV can be determined, as the accuracy of classification is dependent not only on the cover type we wish to classify, but also on the relative position of other cover types within the feature space. It would seem reasonable to conclude on the basis of present evidence that the minimum accurately classifiable area is likely to be between 30 and 56 pixels, for areal units with comparable widths and lengths. In other words, we should multiply the IFOV by between 5.5 and 7.5 to obtain the linear dimensions of the

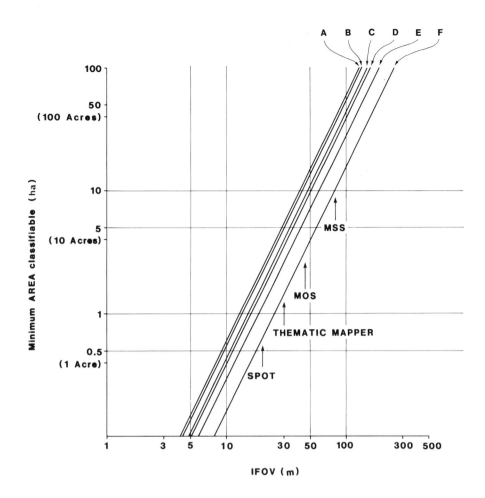

Figure 5   Relationship between the minimum size of area classifiable and the instantaneous field of view. For derivation of lines see text. Data from: A – Shay et al. (1975); B – see text; C – Viglione et al. (1975); D – see text; E – Shay et al. (1975); F – General Electric (1975)

smallest area accurately classifiable. It should be stressed that this does not mean that smaller areal units will not be visually perceptible on imagery. As we have already discussed, subpixel sized areas may be identifiable if they have a sufficiently strong signal. The values quoted above refer to the size of areal units which need to be achieved when dealing with the usual range of spectral responses found in common cover types.

CHOOSING AN APPROPRIATE RESOLUTION

It should be clear from the previous discussion that the improved spatial resolving power of future Earth resources satellites will undoubtedly bring benefits by widening the range of applications and terrain types which can be effectively mapped and monitored. However, improvements will not be won simply by applying current procedures of classification, especially because of the problem of scene noise. Whatever procedure is used for classification, higher resolution imagery may introduce grave problems of data handling. First there are the difficulties of handling data at ground receiving stations, converting these data into usable computer compatible tapes and photographic products and then archiving the data. There is the additional problem of processing the data in order to extract information. This will also be increased substantially with the introduction of higher resolution satellite sensors. Already with the current Landsat MSS, there are serious problems of data handling for many applications. As an illustration, let us note the task of monitoring vegetation conditions in the Sahel. This would seem to be an obvious task to which satellite imagery could contribute. We find that conservatively we would need to analyse some 150 Landsat frames each with more than 200×10^6 bits of data. Any form of computer processing would be very expensive and time-consuming, even assuming that complete Landsat MSS coverage could be obtained regularly. For this and other very broad scale tasks, current Landsat MSS data have a resolution which is much too fine. Recent research suggests that meteorological satellite data with spatial resolutions of 1.1 km may provide a more appropriate technology for such tasks (Townshend & Tucker 1981; Tucker *et al.* 1982).

It will probably never be possible to define the ideal resolving power of satellite sensors. Different applications and different types of terrain and vegetation cover will all affect the resolution we ideally need from satellites. Often the resolutions required may be so high that satellites are unlikely to provide suitable data in the foreseeable future. But for many applications, satellite data will prove suitable. It is incumbent on us to learn how to use such data effectively and efficiently - in the future this will increasingly involve us in correctly choosing from the several sets of satellite imagery with very different resolving powers.

REFERENCES

CLARK, J. & BRYANT, N.A. 1977. Landsat-D thematic mapper simulation using aircraft multi-spectral data. *Proc. int. Symp. Remote Sens. Environ., 11th, Ann Arbor, Michigan,* 483-491.

FRASER, R.S. 1974. Computed atmosphere corrections for satellite data. In: *Scanners and imagery; systems for earth observation,* 64-72. *Proc. Soc. Photo-Optical Engineerings* no. 51.

GENERAL ELECTRIC. 1975. *Definition of total earth resources system for the shuttle era.* (TOS-TERSSE Operational Study 10). Valley Forge, Pa: General Electric.

KAN, E.P., BALL, D.L., BASU, J.P. & SMELSER, R.L. 1975. Data resolution versus forestry classification accuracy. *Symp. Machine Processing of Remotely Sensed Data,* 1B-24 - 1B-36. West Lafayette, Indiana: Purdue University, Laboratory for the Application of Remote Sensing.

LANDGREBE, P.A., BIEHL, L. & SIMMONS, W. 1977. An empirical study of scanner system parameters. *IEEE Trans. Geosci. Electron. (Inst. Elec & Electron. Eng.), GE-15,* 120-130.

LAUER, D.T. & THAMAN, D.R. 1971. Information content of simulated space photographs as a function of various levels of image resolution. *Proc. int. Symp. Remote Sens. Environ., 7th, Ann Arbor, Michigan,* 1191-1203.

MARKHAM, B.L. & TOWNSHEND, J.R.G. 1981. Land cover classification as a function of sensor spatial resolution. *Proc. int. Symp. Remote Sens. Environ., 15th, Ann Arbor, Michigan,* 1075-1090.

SADOWSKI, F.A. & SARNO, J. 1976. *Forest classification accuracy as influenced by multi-spectral scanner spatial resolution.* Report No. 109600-71F. Ann Arbor, Michigan: Environmental Research Institute.

SHAY, R., POTTER, A., BAUER, M., BERSTEIN, R., HARALICK, R., KOSO, A. & SALOMONSON, V. 1975. Appendix F, Subgroup 2 Report. In: *Landsat-D thematic mapper technical working group final report,* edited by J. Harnage and D. Landgrebe (JSC-09797). Houston, Texas: NASA.

SLATER, P.N. 1980. Author's response (to article by Colvocoresses, 1980, in same issue). *Photogramm. Eng. & Remote Sens., 46,* 767-769.

SWAIN, P.H. & DAVIS, S.M. 1978. *Remote sensing: the quantitative approach.* New York: McGraw-Hill.

THOMSON, F.J., ERICKSON, J.D., NALEPKA, R.F. & WEBER, F. 1974. *Final report multi-spectral scanner data applications evaluation. Vol. 1. User applications study.* Rep. No. 102800-40-1. Ann Arbor, Michigan: Environmental Research Institute Michigan.

TOWNSHEND, J.R.G., 1981a. The spatial resolving power of Earth resources satellites. *Prog. Phys. Geogr.,* 5, 32-55.

TOWNSHEND, J.R.G., 1981b. Image analysis and interpretation for land resources survey. In: *Terrain analysis and remote sensing,* edited by J.R.G. Townshend, 59-108. London: Allen & Unwin.

TOWNSHEND, J.R.G. & JUSTICE, C.O. 1981. Information extraction from remotely sensed data. A user view. *Int. J. Remote Sens.,* 2, 313-329.

TOWNSHEND, J.R.G. & TUCKER, C.J. 1981. Utility of imagery from the AVHRR's of NOAA 6 and 7 for vegetation mapping. *Matching remote sensing technologies and their applications past and future. Proc. Ann. Conf. Remote Sens. Soc., 9th, London, 1981,* 97-109. Reading: University of Reading, Remote Sensing Society.

TUCKER, C.J., GATLIN, J., SCHNEIDER, R. & KUCHINOS, M.A. 1982. Monitoring large scale vegetation dynamics in the Nile Delta and River Valley from NOAA AVHRR data. *Proc. Conf. Remote Sensing of arid and semi-arid lands, Cairo, 1982.* in press.

VIGLIONE, S., THOMSON, F., EBERT, D., HOFFER, R., NORWOOD, V. WIGTON, W. & CHEESMAN, G. 1975. Appendix 9, Subgroup 3 report. In: *Landsat-D thematic mapper technical working group final report,* edited by J. Harnage and D. Landgrebe (JSC-09797). Houston, Texas: NASA.

WIERSMA, D.J. & LANDGREBE, D.A. 1978. *The analytical design of spectral measurements from multispectral remote sensor systems.* (LARS Technical Report 122678). West Lafayette, Indiana: Laboratory for the Application of Remote Sensing.

V IMAGE ANALYSIS & DATA DISPLAY

INTERPRETATION AND AUTOMATED MAPPING OF AIRBORNE AND SATELLITE IMAGERY USING THE MACAULAY MAPIP SYSTEM

P F S RITCHIE AND G C STOVE

The Macaulay Institute for Soil Research, Craigiebuckler, Aberdeen

ABSTRACT

The Macaulay Automated Photogrammetric and Interactive Image Processing System is described. The inter-relations between the hardware components, comprising a Wild B8S Stereoplotter, Ferranti System-4 Digitizer, Commodore PET microcomputer, Data General Eclipse computer and Tektronix 4027 colour graphics terminal, are presented in terms of the supporting software. Two software packages are, at present, in course of development. The first allows data digitized from a number of sources, including air photography, airborne multispectral imagery and cartographic material to be processed. These data may be displayed either on- or off-line. The second provides the means for extraction, storage, numerical processing and display of data from Landsat computer compatible tapes. Software designed for specific applications is described and some recent results are presented. Plans for future development are outlined.

INTRODUCTION

Recent years have witnessed a growing interest in the application of micro and mainframe computers to thematic and topographic mapping problems. This paper aims to describe the Macaulay Automated Photogrammetric and Interactive Image Processing (MAPIP) System for processing and presentation of peat and other terrain resource survey data. It will demonstrate the value of computer-assisted techniques for the analysis, display and cartographic output of data derived from ground, air and space.

The use of these facilities is demonstrated by reference to a number of Macaulay studies involving, for example:

1. Thermal linescan survey of Aberdeen
2. Digitizing peat survey data
3. Topographic mapping in Spitsbergen
4. Land classification in Buchan
5. Photogrammetry
6. Air survey data
7. Landsat data analysis

Before discussing these, it is necessary to consider the hardware facilities available.

HARDWARE (Figure 1)

Computer systems

Two computer systems are employed:

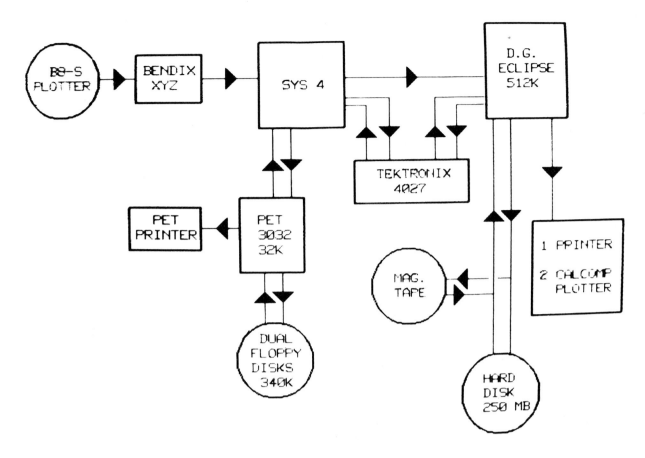

Figure 1   Hardware interconnections within the MAPIP System

1.   The Commodore PET model 3032 microcomputer, with a 32K-byte random access memory, uses a dual-drive floppy disk backing store with a storage capacity of 170K-bytes per disk. The PET is programmed using the BASIC language via an interpreter. In addition, the PETGRAPH high resolution graphics package is used for real time display of digitized data. A Commodore dot programmable monotone graphic printer provides hard copy.

2.   The Data General (DG) Eclipse mainframe computer is operated in time sharing mode and is accessed via the Tektronix colour graphics terminal. The computer has a 512K-byte core memory, with a total of 250M-bytes hard disk backing store. It may be programmed using FORTRAN IV, FORTRAN V (RATFOR) or BASIC language.

Tektronix 4027

This is a terminal which allows data to be displayed using a comprehensive series of hard-wired functions. These include pattern definition, polygon fill-in, vector and circle graphics, and colour selection from a palette of 64 basic hues and shades. Eight colours can be used simultaneously but, with the use of the pattern definition facility, the number of available shades has been increased to 92. The polygon fill-in facility has been employed extensively in thematic representations of digitized and Landsat acquired data.

The 4027 makes available 32K-bytes of input buffer storage and 198K-bytes of addressable graphic storage. Thus, up to 4 screen frames of graphic data can be retained by the declaration of successive graphics areas. Therefore, the possible scrolling area, resulting from the single screen dimensions of 640 x 462 addressable elements, is 640 screen elements horizontally and 1848 vertically.

The display stability of the 4027 unit allows high quality hard copy to be produced by photographing the screen. For colour negative work, a tripod-mounted Hasselblad 500 EL/M camera is used, normally with Kodak 120 125 ASA film. Colour transparencies are obtained using a similarly-mounted Nikon camera with 200 ASA professional film. Black and white displays are possible, again using the pattern definition facility, thus eliminating the necessity for expensive colour reproduction when not required.

Wild B8S Stereoplotter

This instrument allows full geometrical restitution of stereo air photograph pairs for cartographic and thematic purposes. Thus, compensation can be made for tip, tilt and skew distortions between photographs, and scale calibration can be carried out against any required height datum. Cartographic information is conveyed to the PET or Eclipse via the Ferranti Cetec System 4 microprocessor (Stove & Robertson 1980). This uses a Bendix electronic board consisting of a fine matrix of electronic elements permitting a high maximum spatial resolution. The moving cursor contains an electromagnetic detector which transmits positional signals to the System 4.

HARDWARE INTERCONNECTIONS

The Bendix electronic board is positioned on the plotting area of the B8S which has been modified to incorporate electronic detectors which transfer, simultaneously, co-ordinates to the System 4. The PET, at present, is the principal means of processing the digitized data, which can be displayed immediately, either on its high resolution graphics screen or on the Tektronix. Two direct data links exist with the Eclipse computer. The first allows digitized data from the System 4 to be processed and stored by the computer. The second permits the transfer of Landsat data from the Eclipse to the 4027 for display. With the use of software, it is possible to establish a data link between the PET and the Eclipse, by means of a hard-wired Tektronix screen interrogation facility.

MAPIPS SOFTWARE - PHILOSOPHY

MAPIPS is a hybrid system requiring the use of software to link its various components. Originally, the B8S plotter/System 4 Digitizer combination was employed with an IBM 1130 and System 7 computer to produce a data bank on peat and other terrain resources. The subsequent links to the PET, Tektronix 4027 and the DG Eclipse have introduced new possibilities in data processing and display. At present, the principal language used for processing of digitized data is BASIC, and that for Landsat data FORTRAN V (RATFOR). The original Landsat software is well documented (eg McKay & Stove 1980). The BASIC language provides, for the present, a satisfactory link between the PET, the System 4 and the Tektronix. The BASIC interpreter, although slow, is sufficiently rapid to match the speed of display on the Tektronix screen.

Thus, 2 software packages have evolved, with more recent developments concentrating on the microcomputer as a controller for the system. At each stage of development, application to specific projects has been an important factor in software design.

SOFTWARE - MICROCOMPUTER APPLICATIONS

The PET has been utilized for software development in 4 principal fields:

1. Data capture, editing and processing.
2. Data display.
3. Aids to photogrammetry.
4. Air survey applications.

The emphasis at all stages has been on the application of computer methods to current projects. Some of those which have influenced the development of in-house microcomputer software are as follows:

1. *Thermal linescan survey*

Europe's first city-wide airborne thermal linescan survey was conducted over Aberdeen on 11 December 1980. This took the form of a series of parallel transects flown over the city at night in order to detect emitted infrared radiation. The object was to determine the location of highest heat loss from industrial and domestic premises, and agricultural areas. Simultaneous ground measurements were made, and software was developed for the presentation of the resulting data. The methodology used for the processing and display of the thermal infrared data has been described elsewhere (Adams & Ritchie 1981).

2. *Digitizing peat survey data*

A data base covering selected Scottish peatland sites has been established for statistical analysis and cartographic representation of spatial information (Stove & Robertson 1980). The results can be displayed on the Tektronix or on the Calcomp drum plotter. By suitable software design, these data can be viewed in various ways. Results of pollen analysis comprise part of the data base and the MAPIP system has been used to extract and display this information. Distribution maps have been produced which illustrate the relative frequency of selected pollen types preserved during periods of peat formation from the late Glacial to the present.

3. *Topographic mapping - Spitsbergen*

Photogrammetric mapping of selected raised beach deposits and other ice-related phenomena in Spitsbergen was carried out with a view to determining former shoreline elevations and, hence, the isostatic uplift of the area.

4. *Land classification in Buchan*

This survey was carried out in collaboration with Grampian Regional Council with the aim of producing a small scale land cover map which could be utilized for strategic planning purposes (Stove *et al.* 1980). A combination of computer processing of Landsat imagery and visual interpretation using ground truth from selected test areas resulted in a data set suitable for processing and display on the colour terminal. A 'grid' technique, producing regularly spaced geographical information, was employed.

5. *Photogrammetric aids*

Development of the software is ongoing and is intended to aid in the orientation of photogrammetric stereomodels for automated cartography. The microcomputer is currently employed for the implementation of rapid relative and absolute orientation routines, thus affording a substantial saving in time and effort.

6.   Air survey data

Routines have been developed to assist in the processing of data on all air survey sorties. A text editor enables the storage of information related to mission aim, flightpath details, photographic parameters and results.

SOFTWARE - DESCRIPTION

Seventeen routines are described in terms of their applications to the 6 projects described above. They fall into the following 5 groups (Table 1):

TABLE 1   Microcomputer software routines - summary

	Title	Function
Group 1	I/O/E	Input, output and edit digitized data
	DIST/AREA/CIRCLE	Computes distances, areas and circle parameters
	AREA 2	Computes area using triangle summation
	N/BOURS	Calculates nearest neighbour nodal values
Group 2	PATTERNS	Tektronix pattern definition and selection
	GRAPH	Comprehensive graph/histogram presentation
	PLOT 1	Multipurpose data display
	T/SECT	Transect profile presentation
	NET	3-dimensional net display of digitized data
	PIX	Pixel presentation of land cover data
	PLOT 2	Plotting of nearest neighbour data
Group 3	REL/ORIEN	Aid to BS8 relative orientation
	ABS/ORIEN	Aid to absolute orientation
Group 4	INTERVAL	Calculation of stereophoto timing intervals
	MISSIONS	Storage and retrieval of air survey sortie information
Group 5	MENU	Prototype facility utilizing System 4 digitizer
	REF	Keyword reference sorting routine

Group 1

Group 1 includes 4 programs used for data input, manipulation and storage prior to presentation.

Routine 1 is designed to accept data either from the digitizer or from the PET keyboard, and presents options for screen or for line editing. An auto-editing facility has been included in the routine whereby the most common omissions are automatically allowed for. Real time graphics can be presented using the PET high resolution screen, thus enabling the user to keep a continuous record of the area which has been digitized. The routine has been applied specifically to projects 1-5 described above.

Routines 2 & 3 accept digitized data either in real time or from floppy disk, and perform distance and area calculations.

Routine 4 was developed specifically for use in connection with the Aberdeen Thermal Infrared Survey previously described. Data gathered from 15 ground survey stations during the 3 hr mission gave details of weather and, in particular, temperature changes. The program accepted both temperature data and digitized spatial data, which defined station location, and calculated nearest neighbour data for a regular matrix. This information was subsequently reformatted into a form suitable for either a 2-dimensional plot, or a 3-dimensional net model presenting the same basic information as a relief map of the city.

Group 2

Group 2 includes 7 routines specifically intended to allow as much choice as possible when utilizing the Tektronix display for data presentation.

Routine 1 is always invoked prior to using the Tektronix. The hard wired PATTERN command previously described is used to store a set of pattern options in the visual display unit's random access memory. Each pattern is composed of 2 colours, and may consist of 25%, 50%, 75% or 100% of either colour. The 92 patterns currently used result from combinations of the 8 colours simultaneously available. This routine includes an option whereby a sequence of 'hot-to-cold' (white-red-blue) patterns is automatically stored. This option was developed for use whilst plotting Thermal Infrared Survey data. A subroutine allows the selection of any pattern sequence in order to match the requirements. The resulting sequence of pattern reference numbers can be used, for instance, when displaying Landsat data.

Figure 2   *Isopollen contours for pine (Zone VIII) showing a quadratic fit of data from 92 sites. Pollen content increases from south to north*

Routine 2 provides a comprehensive facility for display of numeric data in graphical or histogram form. Size, screen position and resolution can be controlled, allowing the possibility of multiple plots. This routine employs pattern software. Once again, the Thermal Infrared Survey of Aberdeen set many of the specifications for the application of this routine.

Routine 3 is the current flexible utility program used for multipurpose plotting of digitized data. Vector or polygon fill-in plots may be carried out. A superimposition option is included for use in contour overlaying (Figure 2). In particular, this routine has been developed for the display of peat resource data (Figure 3), thermal infrared ground survey data and topographic data derived from photogrammetric plotting of Spitsbergen aerial photographs.

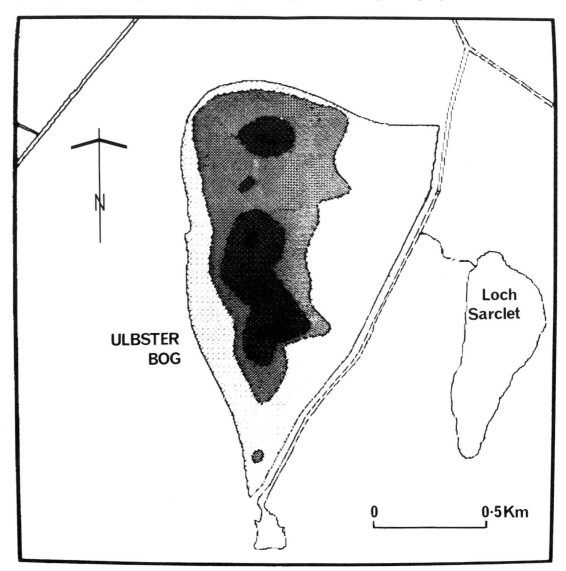

Figure 3   Tektronix 4027 presentation of digitized data representing peat depth contours (isopachytes) within Ulbster Bog, Caithness. Deeper deposits are shown as darker tones

Routine 4 was developed to plot transects across selected Spitsbergen raised beach deposits (Figure 4).

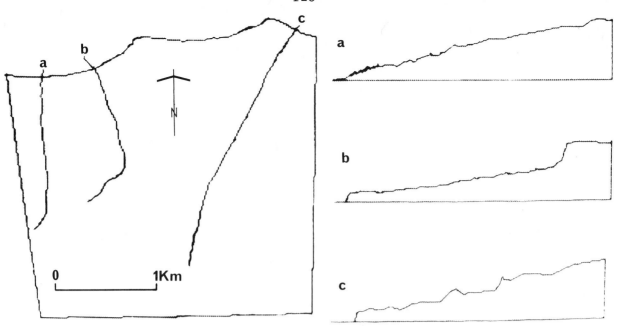

*Figure 4   Plan views and profiles of 3 transects of Spitsbergen raised
beach deposits. Magnification of vertical scale = x10*

Routine 5 is the primary program employed for the 3-dimensional net representation of digitized or manually entered data. Patterns may be selected which
distinguish between x- and y-axes.   The viewing angle may be set at any angle
between 0° (horizontal) and 90°. Azimuth is also variable. The result is the
establishment of optimum values for the presentation of any data set. This
routine has been applied to peat resource data (Figure 5), and temperature
measurements made during the Aberdeen Thermal Infrared Survey.

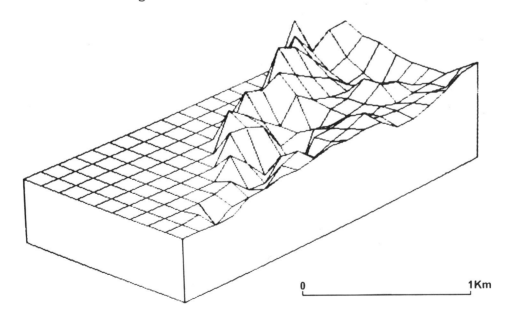

*Figure 5   Three-dimensional net survey representation of peat resource data
obtained by ground survey of Ulbster Bog, Caithness. Magnification of vertical scale = x5*

Routine 6 plots thematic data by colour pattern change. The primary use has
been in the presentation of land cover classification data (Figure 6) and land
use capability information. Up to 32 classes may be defined using the 'pattern'
facility. This routine also utilizes the PET graphic printer for the production
of hard copy output. This peripheral is dot-programmable and thus allows a
purpose-built suite of characters to be defined.

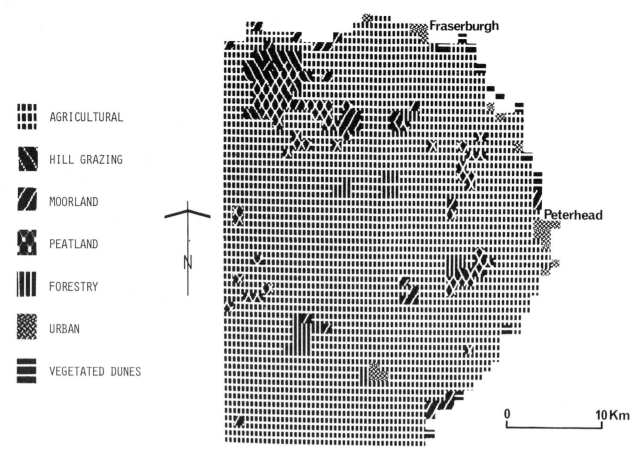

▦	AGRICULTURAL
▧	HILL GRAZING
▨	MOORLAND
▩	PEATLAND
▥	FORESTRY
▤	URBAN
▬	VEGETATED DUNES

*Figure 6   Land cover classification of the Buchan area, Grampian Region,
using digitized data.   The ground resolution was 1 km*

Routine 7 was developed from Routine 6 in order to facilitate the 2-dimensional presentation of nearest neighbour data derived from the Aberdeen thermal linescan survey. Subsequent to the determination of nodal values, the data must be reformatted before display.

Group 3

Group 3 software consists of 2 routines designed to assist in the orientation and calibration of the Wild B8S stereoplotter.

Routine 1 is an aid to the relative orientation of aerial photographs. Mutual corrections to the spatial positions of the photographs relative to each other must be made in order to compensate for differences in the pitch, roll and yaw axes of the aircraft which flew the mission. Using a set of 6 control points, parallax can be eliminated iteratively in each axis, the end result being a pair of perfectly relatively aligned photographs. During this procedure, previously a manual one, digitized data can be processed by the PET and changes in stereoplotter tip and tilt parameters calculated.

Routine 2 enables the user to decrease the time required to orient the stereoplotter with respect to control point height data. This absolute orientation entails an iterative series of triangulations based on a minimum of 3 control points in order that the stereomodel may be calibrated relative to a fixed datum level. Once again, digitized data constitute input to the PET, and common tip, tilt and skew parameters the output. The result is a fully oriented and calibrated stereomodel prepared for either automated or manual cartographic output. These 2 programs save time in model preparation, thus increasing the potential output rate.

Group 4

Group 4 routines are specialized in the processing of air survey data.

Routine 1 has provided comprehensive intervalometer data for use when vertical stereo photography is required. A movable trolley on board a light aircraft carries either one Hasselblad camera or twin Nikons bracketted together. If stereo overlap is required between successive frames, the time interval must be calculated to give the required overlap at a predetermined scale with known aircraft ground speed. Tables have been produced and are in regular use.

Routine 2 is a utility program providing the means of storing, editing and outputting data on all air survey sorties flown to date. Sections covering photographic specifications, flight path details and general administrative information are included.

Group 5

Group 5 consists of 2 miscellaneous routines.

Routine 1 is currently under development as a 'menu' facility for use with the digitizer system. It is anticipated that this will be extended to cover choice of software groups and routines or subroutines within groups. By simple use of the System 4 cursor, it will be possible to select and activate the required software by the touch of a button, thus simplifying the use of the MAPIP system. In this way, the software facility will be consolidated as a cross referenced package which will be more convenient to use and update. The variety of projects for which the system has been utilized has required development in many directions and, by use of menu linkages, a more manageable system should result.

Routine 2 provides a facility for the storage of literature reference keyword data. A database is currently under development which will allow the user to search over 6000 references for any combination of up to 10 keywords. This facility uses the PET floppy disk store to hold and access the data and has been devised specifically to assist investigations in the field of peat research and development.

The description of the 5 groups given above is intended to indicate the wide scope of applications for which a microcomputer may be used in the fields of remote sensing, resource mapping and data presentation.

CURRENT LANDSAT SOFTWARE

Since the installation at the Macaulay Institute of the DG Eclipse, all Landsat software which was developed originally on the Honeywell 66/80 at Aberdeen University Computer Centre has been translated from FORTRAN IV to RATFOR (Table 2). Developments are in progress to adapt selected software to take advantage of the plotting options available on the Tektronix. In particular, 2 are briefly described.

1. The pattern facility has allowed an increasing number of density slices to be applied to Landsat Computer Compatible Tapes (CCT) reflectance data. After

studying the output from HISTOGRAM, which uses input data from a previously extracted portion of a selected Landsat CCT, the user defines a classification using CLASSES and, having utilized the PET pattern select facility to define a colour sequence, plots the result (Table 2).

2. The ability to use the existing software to study resampled CCTs (that is, those which have been modified with respect to either geometry or radiometric calibration) is becoming increasingly important as precision-corrected tapes become available.

TABLE 2   Landsat software - summary

Title	Function
HEADER	Reads CCT information
AREA	Sets limits of required extract from Landsat CCT
FORT	Extracts data from CCT using information held in AREA
PREBEST	Prepares histograms from extracted data
HISTOGRAM	Presents histograms for interpretation and subsequent classification
CLASSES	Permits user input of classification data
QUICKMAP	Establishes data file from extract in a form suitable for line printer or Tektronix output Uses data in CLASSES
SHADE	Provides printer output from QUICKMAP data
TSHADE	Provides Tektronix output from QUICKMAP data using 8 colours
TSHD62	Provides Tektronix output from QUICKMAP data using up to 62 colour patterns

FUTURE DEVELOPMENTS

The recent acquisition of a Wild Aviotab TA flatbed cartographic plotting table, together with a tri-axis locator for the B8S stereoplotter, will enable high quality topographic and thematic hard copy output. The locator, by transmitting data in 3 dimensions to the table, will perform a function similar to that of the System 4 digitizer and encoder. Computer links from the latter to the PET and the Eclipse will make data processing and storage possible.

In the short term, it is intended that principal software advances will be oriented towards the establishment of a flexible cartographic output facility.

CONCLUSIONS

Remote sensing techniques are being increasingly used in resource mapping and related applications. Some examples of project oriented software development have been described, demonstrating the use of a hybrid photogrammetric and image processing system. Emphasis has been placed on software flexibility, and the expectation that established routines will be of use in future applications. An outline of future system development is described and, in particular, the expected increased capability in hard copy cartographic output

REFERENCES

ADAMS, M.J. & RITCHIE, P.F.S. 1981. Processing and analysis of thermographic data with the aid of a microcomputer. *Comput. Appl. (Nott.)*, 7, 973-993.

McKAY, D.A.P. & STOVE, G.C. 1980. Digital processing and analysis of Landsat MSS data (Fucino CCTs) on a Honeywell 66/80 Computer. *Comput. Appl. (Nott.)*, 6, 936-995.

STOVE, G.C. & ROBERTSON, R.A. 1980. Development of photogrammetric and remote sensing techniques for peat and land use surveys in Scotland. *Telma*, 10, 67-82. (In German).

STOVE, G.C., BIRNIE, R.V., CAIRNS, J.G. & RITCHIE, P.F.S. 1980. *Land use survey of Buchan based on satellite remote sensing*. Report to the Grampian Region Department of Physical Planning. Aberdeen: Macaulay Institute for Soil Research.

ANALYSIS OF REMOTELY SENSED DATA ON THE NERC I^{2}S SYSTEM

J R BAKER

Experimental Cartography Unit, Natural Environment Research Council, Swindon

ABSTRACT

The image analysis system at the Experimental Cartography Unit in Swindon is a facility for the use of scientists from NERC Institutes and NERC funded university groups. The system is described in some detail and its capabilities are illustrated through a specific ecological example, an investigation of Landsat imagery of Cumbria to determine the vegetation mapping capabilities of the multi-spectral data.

INTRODUCTION

In December 1980, the Scientific Services section of the Natural Environment Research Council (NERC) placed an order for a System 101 image processing system with International Imaging Systems (I^{2}S) of Sunnyvale, California. The I^{2}S processor, with its Hewlett-Packard (HP) computer and associated software system, was installed in the Experimental Cartography Unit (ECU), Wingate House, Swindon at the end of March and went into operation at the beginning of April 1981.

The I^{2}S System 101 is a well proven and fully integrated hardware and software system for the fast and flexible interactive processing of all types of digital image data in both a research and production environment. Being a complete turnkey system, it was able to conduct effective image processing immediately after acceptance, with no lengthy period of hardware assembly and software development. The major elements are described in the first 4 sections which cover the Hewlett-Packard system, the I^{2}S processor, the Optronics Colourwriter and the System 101 software package. In the following sections the characteristics of Landsat imagery are noted, and the analysis of these data on the I^{2}S system is illustrated by a specific ecological example. In conclusion, the achievements of the system, since its installation, are summarized briefly.

THE HEWLETT-PACKARD SYSTEM

The HP 3000 Series III computer is a general purpose mini computer. It has a 16-bit word, addressing instruction at byte and word level, hardware multiply and divide, and floating point hardware for both 32-bit and 64-bit real numbers. The associated mass storage media comprise 2 1600 bpi, 45 ips, magnetic tape units and 3 120 Mbyte disk units. One HP 2640B terminal unit is the main terminal for image analysis work, while an HP 2635B hardcopy unit is employed as the system console. The HP 3000 computer runs under the unaltered Multi Programming Executive (MPE)-III HP operating system, a general disk-based software system which provides powerful virtual memory and timesharing facilities, and supervises the processing of user programs within the central processor. In the multiprogramming environment, several related or unrelated programs are in partial states of completion and resources are allocated amongst them to balance the system load and to meet response and throughput requirements. Each user can employ the computer interactively as though it were a dedicated machine, while a series of batch jobs can run in the background. MPE-III employs stack architecture which automatically provides the separation of data from code and makes all software re-entrant while the dynamic loading of data and code as required gives a virtual memory capability yielding an effective memory space that far exceeds the 512 kbytes of real memory.

The HP 3000 is provided with a FORTRAN 3000 compiler based on ANSI standard FORTRAN, and also a System Programming Language (SPL) compiler which offers the programmer a high-level language similar (but not equivalent) to ALGOL, to produce the more usual coding sequences, but with features that enable him to easily exert control over the machine-dependent functions of the computer system such as interrupt handling and register and bit manipulations.

THE INTERNATIONAL IMAGING SYSTEMS MODEL 70 PROCESSOR

The Model 70 image processor is a complex piece of digital hardware close to the present state-of-the-art in its capability to process large numerical arrays speedily and flexibly. Nevertheless, the concepts upon which it operates are simple enough. The key elements of the Model 70 are the refresh memory channels which hold the data, and the 3 pipeline processors which operate on the data.

Each refresh memory channel is a solid state, dynamic, random access memory (RAM) and stores an array of 512 x 512 elements with 8-bit accuracy, ie 256 levels per pixel. Up to 12 channels of refresh memory can be implemented, although at present only 4 are available. As the refresh memory is random accessible, the host computer can write to or read from any bit within any pixel with minimal wait time. The refresh memory is loaded from the host computer via the input function memory which is a programmable 13-bit to 8-bit look-up table, ie an array of 8192 words (2^{13}) containing values in the range 0 to 225 (2^8-1). For each 13-bit number input, the appropriate array location is accessed and the 8-bit contents output. After the host computer has suitably loaded this look-up table, a whole range of linear and non-linear image transformations can be achieved, eg scaling, negation, logarithmic and anti-logarithmic functions, and histogram equalization.

The requirement of the pipeline processors is that they can process an entire image of 262 144 bytes at full video rates, ie 25 Hz, or at a rate of 8×10^6 pixels per second. The clock rate of the processor is therefore 10 MHz. Each pipeline processor can be broken down into a number of elements. The first set of these is concerned with deriving the addresses in the refresh memory planes of the pixels to be extracted for processing.

1. Image scrolling: each stored image can be displayed with an independent x and y displacement of between 0 and 511 samples and lines.

2. Image zooming: each stored image can be magnified by a factor of 1, 2, 4 or 8. This is achieved, in the case of a zoom of 8 for example, by stepping the address counter in x and y only every eighth sample and every eighth line to provide magnification by pixel replication.

3. Split-screening: arbitrary rectangular portions of various stored images can be displayed simultaneously.

Image scrolling can provide gross registration of images stored in separate refresh memory channels, and is essential to accumulating partial sums during convolution operations. The split-screen facility, combined with scrolling, allows, for example, the display in adjacent quadrants of the monitor screen of identical 256 x 256 windows for 4 bands of the same image, or the display of a 512 x 512 window positioned anywhere in a 1024 x 1024 image whose quadrants are stored in 4 refresh memory channels. Further, in combination with zoom, smaller windows can be displayed at higher magnification.

Having selected the appropriate area of the images from the refresh memories for subsequent processing, the images can be combined with the 4 basic arithmetic functions. This is accomplished by 3 further pipeline elements.

4.   The look-up tables: each pipeline has one 8-bit to 9-bit look-up table for each refresh memory channel, and the output data stream from each look-up table can be selectively enabled or disabled.

5.   The adder array: the transformation to 9-bits enables 2's complement arithmetic to be performed as the adder array sums the outputs from the enabled look-up tables. The range of the output can be up to 13-bits if all 12 refresh planes are implemented. The minimum and maximum values of this summed data stream are used by the host computer to apply a constant offset, usually to bias the data stream towards zero, and then to extract 10 contiguous bits.

6.   The output function memory: this is a single 10-bit to 10-bit look-up table for each pipeline for the real time transformation of the summed data stream.

This basic pipeline architecture of look-up tables, adder array, and output function memory enables addition, subtraction, multiplication and division to be accomplished between images in real time. For example, if positive linear ramps are loaded into look-up tables and output function memory, then the images are added, while if some look-up tables are loaded with negative linear ramps, then those images will be subtracted. Similarly, if the look-up tables are loaded with logarithmic functions and the output function memory is loaded with an exponential function, then the images are multiplied, while if some look-up tables are loaded with negative logarithmic functions, then those images are divided into those with a positive logarithmic function in their look-up table. Dependent on which look-up tables are enabled and which disabled, the output of each of the 3 pipelines is determined by all, some or none of the images in the refresh memory planes, providing thereby very powerful facilities for combining images.

The output function memories present the 3 pipeline outputs to:

1.   The videometer: this calculates in real time the histogram of the 10-bit outputs, either for the entire scene, or for a subarea of the scene defined by a programmable region-of-interest mask in a graphics overlay channel.

2.   The feedback unit: all of the processing is performed within the pipelines on the data stored in the refresh memory, but the original data remain unchanged. With the feedback unit, however, the results of processing can be returned to the refresh memory for subsequent processing by the Model 70, for example in an iterative loop, or for subsequent transfer to the host computer.

3.   The colour monitor: the outputs of the red, green and blue pipeline processing channels drive 3 digital to analogue converters to control the primary output medium of the Model 70, a high precision Mitsubishi 19 inch colour monitor.

For overlaying of the image with binary data, an array of up to 8 independent one-bit data memories can be implemented; 4 such graphics planes are presently available. They are used to display the system status, or to hold region-of-interest masks, histograms and cumulative histograms, alphanumeric notation, maps and overlays, etc. The intensity of each graphics plane is determined by a 5-bit number for each primary colour, yielding a total palette of 32 768 displayable colours. This ensures that the individual graphics planes are always separable, even if they superimpose one another on the screen in a complex way. A programmable cursor is also available as a pseudo-graphics overlay. Its position is determined by the x and y location registers which can either be set by a program in the host computer or by the operator using the trackball as an input device.

THE OPTRONICS C-4300 COLOURWRITER

The intermediate processing results on the I²S system can either be sent to the Versatec V80 printer-plotter if monochrome hard-copy output is satisfactory, or can be photographed directly off the Mitsubishi colour monitor screen using a 35 mm camera. However, for the production of publication-quality results, and in particular large format slides, the Optronics C-4300 Colourwriter can be employed. Data are transferred as byte images written line by line on an 800 or 1600 bpi multifile magnetic tape in a band sequential format for offline plotting on the Optronics. Five spot sizes can be selected (25, 50, 100, 200 or 400 microns) over a film of 25 x 25 cm. The Optronics is capable of plotting in black and white or, by sequential exposure through manually selected red, green and blue filters, in colour. The associated dark room is equipped with a Colenta processor for developing sheet and roll film, a contact printer and a Durst colour enlarger for Cibachrome prints.

THE SYSTEM 101 SOFTWARE PACKAGE

Running within the standard MPE-III HP operating system and employing many HP provided functions are the image processing operating system and the applications software which together constitute the I²S System 101 package.

The I²S image processing operating and management system is specifically designed to facilitate the manipulation of images. For example,

1. the image data can be kept in several different forms, bit, byte, integer, real, double precision, complex, and even long complex.

2. The one-dimensional array in which the multidimensional image data are stored can be organized in virtually any manner and have up to 8 dimensions (of which the applications software normally only uses 4). Two of these dimensions are usually spatial x/column/sample and y/row/line, and the others can be, for example, spectral (for multispectral scanner data), temporal (for a series of data acquisition dates), polarization, or stereo.

3. The images can be stored on computer compatible tapes, HP disks or I²S refresh memory planes.

Two image directories are kept for each S101 user to manage his data, one consisting of online images immediately accessible from disk and the other of offline images stored on magnetic tape.

An image to be processed can be subsectioned and subsampled in order, for example, to reduce its size to 512 x 512 bytes for display purposes, and it can be subbanded to extract the required spectral or temporal bands for processing.

For efficiency reasons, most of the image processing operating system is coded in SPL, but the applications software is coded in FORTRAN IV in order to simplify updates and future changes and to make the programs more readily understandable. The applications programs are of two distinct types, central processor unit (CPU) programs which use only the HP computer and produce a mathematically accurate result, and display programs which offload some of the computations from the host computer to the Model 70 image processor for specialized high speed analysis and may produce a linearly scaled result. This local processing is especially useful to interpretative analysis because the speed and response are much greater than can be achieved using the host computer alone.

The image processing operating system can support many users of the System 101 both in batch and in interactive mode. Each user has command stacks for system, CPU and display commands. System commands run very quickly and are executed immediately they are typed in. CPU commands may execute for a considerable time, and they are put into a stack, a particular command only running when all previously typed commands have completed. Display commands have a stack like CPU commands, but only one user at any time can actually use the Model 70 image processor. Thus, the System 101 in general and the system and CPU commands in particular constitute a multi-user system, but the display commands constitute a single-user system. A new user must wait until the present user has released the Model 70 before he can acquire it for his own display commands.

A help file is available to provide online documentation for all applications functions. Furthermore, new applications programs can frequently be created by employing an existing applications program as a skeleton, and using the I^2S augmented version of the EDIT 3000 HP text editor to make the necessary changes to the FORTRAN code.

CHARACTERISTICS OF LANDSAT IMAGERY

The Landsat series of Earth resource satellites was launched by the US National Aeronautics and Space Administration (NASA) in the 1970s. They are at a nominal height of 910 km in sun synchronous near polar orbits. The multi-spectral scanner (MSS) sweeps in a direction perpendicular to the satellite track over 1/5th of a radian about the nadir, yielding a swath width of 180 km. Thus, during a satellite overpass, an entire image of the scene below is gradually built up from the individual scans. The MSS has 4 spectral bands, band 4 (0.5-0.6 μm), band 5 (0.6-0.7 μm), band 6 (0.7-0.8 μm), and band 7 (0.8-1.1 μm), corresponding to visible green, visible red, and 2 near infrared channels. To speed the acquisition of data, each band has 6 individual sensors, but this can give rise to 6 line striping on the images if the sensors' relative alignments are not accurate. The nominal resolution of the MSS is an instantaneous field of view of 79 m, and adjacent scan lines are separated by 79 m. However, the data are sampled at a rate corresponding to a separation in the sampling direction of 56 m, so that the image has a non-unit aspect ratio and adjacent samples tend to be more highly correlated than adjacent lines. The orbit is such that a given scene is acquired on an 18 day repeat cycle at a local mean time of about 0930.

The most recent satellite of the series, Landsat-3, also has a Return Beam Videcon (RBV) camera on board forming a 2-dimensional image on an array of sensors which is then read off digitally. The RBV camera is a wide band monochromatic sensor having a spatial resolution of 30 m, rather finer than the MSS. Having due regard to the different geometric characteristics of the 2 imaging systems, it is possible to accurately register MSS and RBV data. By deriving an image in which the RBV channel determines the intensity while the 4 MSS channels determine the hue and saturation, the high spatial resolution of the RBV camera can be combined with the spectral resolution of the MSS. However, the intensive image processing task involved, coupled with instrumental problems on the RBV camera itself, has thus far prevented this from becoming a standard technique.

In the UK, European Landsat imagery can be acquired from the National Point of Contact of Earthnet at the Royal Aircraft Establishment (RAE), Farnborough. RAE has a large archive of UK scenes and can order anything additional from the European Space Agency. Non European Landsat imagery can be acquired direct from the Earth Resources Observation System (EROS) Data Centre at Sioux Falls, South Dakota, USA. The Landsat magnetic tape library associated with the I^2S consists of one set of raw data for each Landsat scene covering the British Isles, plus one set of geometrically corrected data tabulated at 50 m resolution as generated by RAE for the whole UK. In addition, the library contains Landsat scenes on other dates of areas in the UK having a particular interest (eg Snowdonia, Severn Estuary) plus other non European Landsat scenes (eg Botswana, Egypt, Kenya, USA).

The tape index is stored on disk and can be updated using the HP forms entry program VIEW 3000. This index can be interrogated in a useful and flexible way using the keyed sequential access mode (KSAM) HP file system, for example to list the tape numbers ordered by image acquisition data for all imagery held of a particular geographic area.

PROCESSING OF LANDSAT IMAGERY FOR ECOLOGICAL RESEARCH

An investigation of the usefulness of Landsat imagery for ecological mapping in the Lake District provides a good example of the power of the I^2S Image Analysis system. The 4 images on the front cover illustrate this analysis.

The first stage in the investigation is to read the computer compatible tape for the area and date of interest on to disk. One Landsat image of 3248 samples by 2286 lines by 4 bands is approximately 30 Mbytes of data and fills one 1600 bpi magnetic tape. To read these data takes about 10 minutes and it fills a quarter of one of the disk packs. An overview is displayed on the colour monitor by defining a centred window of 3072 samples by 2048 lines and extracting every sixth sample and every fourth line to yield a low resolution 512 x 512 image. The standard way of presenting the 4 independent bands of Landsat in 3 colours is to let bands 7, 5 and 4 determine the intensities of red, green and blue on the colour monitor. This corresponds to the portrayal on colour infrared film where the intensity in each of the 3 visible primary colours on the film is determined by the scene radiances in the colours shifted one band into the infrared. For scenes in temperate latitudes, the result will be a predominantly red image due to the high reflected radiance in the infrared band 7 coming from surface vegetation. The overview enables the position of the area of interest to be specified and an image of size 1024 x 1024 to be extracted. This scene is uncorrected both geometrically and radiometrically. In particular it shows the 6 band striping in the line direction inherent in the MSS. A locally variant analysis to minimize abrupt changes in mean and standard deviation of the pixel radiances within a specified window is used to effectively remove the striping. Then to compensate for skew in the image introduced by earth rotation during the satellite pass, to correct for the aspect ratio of the scanning system and to rotate the image to a co-ordinate frame with north uppermost, the destriped image is transferred by interpolating it on to a new set of lattice points. Three interpolation algorithms are available, nearest neighbour, bilinear using a 2 by 2 neighbourhood, and cubic spline using a 4 by 4 neighbourhood. The computer time required is proportional to the number of pixels constituting the neighbourhood. This transformation provides a rectangular array that is partially filled with the image over an inscribed rectangle. A filled inscribed square 512 by 512 about the area of interest can then be extracted for further processing. This scene is now geometrically corrected to a more normal projection - that of, for example, an aerial photograph taken from a metric camera on board a high flying aircraft. Radiometrically the data encompass virtually the same range as the raw data before destriping.

The intensity ranges covered by the data in the refresh memory planes can be displayed as histograms (and cumulative histograms) of the number of pixels having an intensity equal to (or not greater than) each of the possible 256 intensity levels. As could have been predicted from the image of Cumbria, the histogram shows that the infrared channel only utilizes the lower half of the displayable range, and the visible channels utilize only the lower quarter of this range. In order to utilize the displayable range of 8 bits to the full, a contrast stretch is applied to the data residing in the refresh memory using the look-up tables in the pipeline processors. The same stretch can be applied to all channels, but it is more usual to stretch each channel independently. In a linear stretch, all intensities in the input data equal to or below a lower limit are mapped to the lowest extreme of the output data, and all intensities in the input greater than or equal to the upper limit are mapped to the upper extreme. Intensity values within the limits are linearly interpolated to cover the whole displayable range. The lower limit and upper limit are usually specified from the histogram either as the actual minimum and maximum of the data or as the range of a particular component of the histogram, or as clip levels, eg the intensity which brackets the central 90% of the area under the histogram. In practice, the last of these linear stretches is almost always found to be effect- ive*. Alternatively the slope and intercept of the linear look-up table between the input and output data values can be determined subjectively by the scientist moving the trackball in the x and y directions, rather than objectively from the histograms.

Three forms of non-linear stretch are also available which stretch the data over intensity ranges populated by many pixels and compress the data over intensity ranges populated by few pixels. The look-up table between the input and output intensities can be set up so that the histogram of the output scene is as close as possible to the histogram of another actual image (histogram matching), or a standard image containing one broad Gaussian distribution of pixel intensity values (histogram normalization), or a standard image containing an equal number of pixels at each intensity value (histogram equalization).

It is possible to define a region of interest on a graphics overlay plane and calculate the histogram in the pipeline processor just for the area of the image contained within the mask, in order to extract one component of the scene. Furthermore, the linear and non-linear stretches can also be so restricted so that the statistics used to stretch the entire scene are derived only from the region of interest.

The false colour display of Landsat bands 7, 5 and 4 has made no use of MSS band 6. All 4 bands can be displayed in quadrants of the display screen using a split screen mode. Flickering between bands 6 and 7 does indeed reveal differences between them, indicating that, by omitting band 6 from the previous analysis, infor- mation was being lost. By deriving various statistical parameters from the scene radiances, including the covariance matrix between spectral bands, the eigenvectors can be used to effect a Karhunen-Loewe transformation of the image radiances. In the 4-dimensional space defined by the radiances in each of the Landsat bands, this transformation corresponds to a rotation of co-ordinate axes to the principal axes. The first principal axis is chosen along the direction in feature space of maximum scene variance, and higher order components along orthogonal axes having progressively smaller proportions of the total scene variance†. The choice of wavelength bands for the Landsat sensors is such that, over the UK, bands 4 and 5 are highly correlated, as are bands 6 and 7. The eigenvectors show that the first principal component is almost entirely a combination of bands 6 and 7, while the second component is almost entirely composed of bands 4 and 5. The eigenvalues show that these components contain 0.85 and 0.14 of the total scene variance, leaving very little information to be shared between the third and fourth principal components. This is confirmed when the 4 principal components, as opposed to the 4 observed bands, are displayed in the split screen mode. By this analysis the probability distributions of the clusters in feature space have been

*See cover figure, upper left quadrant   †See cover figure, upper right quadrant

aligned more closely with the axes, and the dimensionality of the data set has been reduced. This speeds the computations in the later analysis in the HP CPU, and is essential for further analysis in the 4 channel Model 70 display processor, where the 2 channels are required as an array of 16-bit accumulators for some of the later processing leaving only 2 channels for the data. By loading these 2 channels with the first and second principal components, almost all the information in the original scene is being utilized.

Having performed this feature space rotation, a 2-dimensional scattergram can be displayed which is a projection of the multidimensional feature space on to a plane containing the first 2 principal axes. In a 2-dimensional plot with the one-dimensional histograms on the borders, the number of pixels in the scene having each possible combination of radiances in the first and second principal components is represented in the z direction by a grey scale. This can, if required, be coded so that each particular range of number of pixels is represented by a unique colour. Areas in the original image having distinct spectral signatures will be represented in this display by distinct clusters in feature space. In the case of Cumbria, the most obvious clusters correspond to clear water, water containing suspended sediment, lowland agricultural areas, and high moorland areas, with many finer surface cover classes such as different vegetative types evident on closer inspection*.

This scattergram can be used as the input to a cluster analysis program which also runs in the Model 70 image computer. Feature space is divided into, say, 16 clusters which are approximately equally populated, each cluster being defined by the mean and standard deviation of radiance for each spectral band. The pixels belonging to each cluster are determined, the mean and standard deviations of their radiances evaluated, and the cluster parameters redefined as a result. After looping around this iterative cycle 8 to 16 times, the process normally converges to a self-consistent net of clusters. In the resulting classification map, a number from 0 to 16 at a particular sample and line number indicates that the pixel radiances at that location in the image had a spectral signature that corresponded most closely to clusters 1 to 16, or did not correspond to any cluster, in which case the position is assigned to reject class 0. This class map can also be colour coded so that regions having the same spectral signature in the original data are represented by the same colour in the class map†. The classification procedure is unsupervised, ie it does not employ any of the scientist's knowledge or prejudice about the various ground cover types in the scene.

All of these techniques,

1.   combining Landsat bands 7, 5 and 4 into a red, green and blue false colour composite and applying a linear or non-linear contrast stretch;

2.   combining principal components 1, 2 and 3 in a similar way;

3.   inspecting the histograms, both in one and 2 dimensions;

4.   performing a cluster analysis,

give the ecologist a feel for the separability or otherwise of the surface vegetation types he wishes to discriminate between in the data from the Landsat MSS acquired on a particular date.

From this point, he will normally proceed to a more sophisticated analysis using additional information to define training areas which supervise the classification algorithms which are available within the System 101 package and which

*See cover figure, lower left quadrant   †See cover figure, lower right quadrant

run in the HP central processor. This comparison with additional data sources will probably also necessitate rubber sheeting the Landsat image to the projection of a particular map, for example the UK National Grid. This entails using the cursor to determine the sample and line numbers on the image of stable high contrast features which can also be recognized on the map and whose Eastings and Northings can be measured accurately. A series of xy co-ordinate pairs in both the original and target co-ordinate frame is then used to determine the matrix transformation between the 2 frames, and the original image is retabulated on to the new lattice to yield an image which exactly registers with the map. In these latter stages, ground control both for geometric accuracy and for classification accuracy is clearly essential to a successful analysis.

CONCLUSION

The NERC I^{2}S System is a powerful tool for the analysis of raster data, usually images acquired from sensors operating in the visible or near infrared parts of the spectrum on board an aircraft or satellite. Thanks to a user-friendly software interface, a visiting scientist can speedily learn to employ the system for effective analysis of data for his own research purposes, using techniques such as linear and non-linear contrast stretches, pseudo-colouration, principal component analysis, geometric rectification and unsupervised and supervised classification. Over the 8 months that the I^{2}S System has been running, a large number of users, both from NERC Institutes and NERC funded university groups, have been trained to a level where they are competent to use it in a hands-on mode, and it has shown its power in the wide range of topics for which it has been employed, not just in ecological mapping but also in geology, geo-chemistry, coastal zone processes and deep ocean wave studies.

VI POSSIBLE TRENDS IN ECOLOGICAL SURVEY

SATELLITE IMAGERY FOR ENVIRONMENTAL RESEARCH - THE NEXT 10 YEARS

M J JACKSON AND J PLEVIN
NERC Scientific Services, Natural Environment Research Council, Swindon

ABSTRACT

The paper provides a brief review of the existing environmental satellites and then describes those approved for launch before 1990. It also examines some of the policy issues which relate to the operational future of such missions.

EARLY DAYS

The idea of looking at the Earth from space in any practical sense goes back as far as the ballistic launches of the Aerobee, Viking and Atlas rockets in the late 1940s and early 1950s. These early suborbital flights prepared the ways for later, manned, USA and USSR missions. The manned missions, whilst of great relevance to the development of the overall space programme, did not, however, emphasize to any great extent the development of Earth observation techniques; the concern was much more towards the idea of lunar landings and establishing manned space stations.

In parallel to the early Gemini and Apollo effort, more sophisticated automatic satellite systems were under development by the US National Aeronautics and Space Administration (NASA), and the first of these of particular relevance to the terrestrial ecologist was Landsat-1, launched in July 1972. This enabled, for the first time, repetitive multispectral images of the Earth's surface to be acquired in a routine manner and for a wide range of applications.

RECENT SATELLITES

The success of the *Landsat* programme has been considerable and Landsats-2 and 3 were launched in 1975 and 1978 respectively. Also, Europe has invested in Landsat through the European Space Agency (ESA) by building ground stations at Fucino in Italy and Kiruna in Sweden. Whilst all 3 satellites have had both a *Multispectral Scanner* (MSS) and *Return Beam Videcon* (RBV) camera on board, only the MSS data have been available in any quantity, though a few RBV images have appeared. The characteristics of these Landsat sensors are well documented elsewhere but some details are presented in Table 1 (see also Tables 3 and 4).

Whilst Landsat has been the most significant satellite for terrestrial scientists, there have been other missions. The *Heat Capacity Mapping Mission* (HCMM) (Table 1) permitted thermal infrared images to be collected over selected areas at 12 hour intervals, and the differences between the day and night images were used to study the thermal properties of near surface materials providing information of use in geology and hydrology.

Satellites for oceanographic applications have also been developed and have included in their payloads a range of microwave sensors that enable rapidly changing phenomena to be observed under all weather conditions. Although the lifetime of *Seasat* (Table 1) was short (100 days), data from the *altimeter* and *scatterometer* indicate very favourably that these sensors are capable of providing accurate measurements of surface wind fields and waves. The high resolution land and sea surface images produced by the Seasat *Synthetic Aperture Radar* (SAR) have received considerable attention, highlighting a number of interesting features and potential application areas.

TABLE 1   Summary characteristics of NASA remote sensing satellites for earth survey, marine and environmental monitoring applications

Satellite	Orbit				Main imaging sensors	Ground resolu-tion/m	No. of spectral bands	Swath/ FOV/km	Other sensors
	Altitude/ km	Incli-nation	Repetit-ion rate	Launch date					
Landsat-1 and 2	920	99	18 days	7/72 & 7/75	MSS RBV	80 80	4 3	185 185 x 185	Data collection
Landsat-3	920	99	18 days	3/78	MSS RBV	80 40	5 1	185 130 x 130	Data collection
HCMM (Heat capacity mapping mission)	600	98	12 hours	4/78	Heat capacity mapping radiometer	500	2	700	–
Seasat	800	108		7/78	SAR SMMR	25 16-144 km (function freq.)	1 5	100 (250-350 off nadir)	1.Radar altimeter 2.Vis/IR Scanner 3.Microwave Scatterometer
Nimbus-7	925	99	2-3 days	10/78	CZCS SMMR	800 Similar to Seasat	6 4	600	

NASA   National Aeronautics and Space Administration   SAR   Synthetic Aperture Radar
MSS   Multispectral Scanner   SMMR   Scanning Multichannel Microwave Radiometer
RBV   Return Beam Videcon   CZCS   Coastal Zone Colour Scanner

The *Coastal Zone Colour Scanner* (CZCS) flown on the *Nimbus-7* satellite (Table 1), and still operating (November 1981) after more than 3 years, has provided data related to chlorophyll concentrations and suspended sediments in near surface coastal and ocean waters. Early experiments have shown that CZCS data are of great interest both to marine biologists, in their studies of productivity, and to physical oceanographers studying ocean fronts and mixing processes between different water types.

The experience gained using data from the first generation of remote sensing satellites has provided the scientific basis and starting point for the development of the new satellite systems described in the next section.

THE NEXT 10 YEARS

The economic depression which has so badly affected the USA and Europe has also had an impact on the future remote sensing programme. In the USA, the major NOSS oceanographic mission has been cancelled and the long term operational future of the Landsat programme remains unclear. Furthermore, the long list of 'hopefuls' defined by NASA and US Agencies in the preceding healthier climate now seems to have only a remote chance of being launched before 1990. Thus, the US Geological Survey defined MAPSAT and the proposed STEREOSAT missions seem unlikely to fly before 1990, and an operational multiple linear array sensor, whilst still an approved development programme, also has no defined launch date.

On the European scene, the originally proposed trio of ESA satellites. LASS, COMSS and GOMSS, which were conceived as Land Applications, Coastal Ocean

Monitoring and Global Ocean Monitoring Satellite Systems, has shrunk to a single approved mission (ERS-1) for ocean monitoring applications. It is unlikely that there will be further major ESA remote sensing satellites before 1990.

It is not intended to present too pessimistic and depressing a note, however. Most of this contraction was inevitable, as early optimistic hopes are translated into funded realities. There is still a programme which is of major interest to environmental scientists and the next section describes the 4 missions given in Table 2.

TABLE 2   Launch programme, to 1990, of satellites of major interest to environmental scientists

Mission	Launch date	Country/Agency
Landsat-D	1982	USA
SPOT	1984	France
MOS-1	1986/7	Japan
ERS-1	1987	ESA

The US Landsat-D* mission continues the highly successful series of Landsat satellites. There are a number of major differences, however (Table 3), the most significant of these being the demise of the RBV cameras and the introduction of the *Thematic Mapper* (TM) which has considerably higher spectral and spatial resolution than the MSS, and improved geometric and radiometric capabilities.

TABLE 3   Comparison of the characteristics of Landsats-1, -2 and -3 with those of Landsat-D

	Landsats-1 & 2	Landsat-3	Landsat-D
Altitude	917 km	917 km	795 km
Repeat cycle	18 days	18 days	16 days
Sensors	MSS, RBV	MSS, RBV	MSS, TM
Spectral bands	4 for MSS 3 for RBV	4 for MSS 1 for RBV	4 for MSS 7 for TM

The characteristics of the TM are compared with MSS in Table 4. The TM is a very exciting development though it has not been without an element of controversy or without problems. The instrument integrated into the satellite includes some minor sensor faults relating to the functioning of certain of the receptor cells, and some loss of data is now to be expected. There has also been controversy over the scanner design sharpened by the French choice of the fixed array or 'push-broom' optical sensor for the SPOT satellite.

*Landsat-D was launched by NASA on 16 July 1982 and is renamed Landsat-4

TABLE 4   Comparisons between MSS and Thematic Mapper (TM)

MSS	Band 1	0.5 – 0.6 μm	
*IFOV =	Band 2	0.6 – 0.7 μm	
80 m	Band 3	0.7 – 0.8 μm	
	Band 4	0.8 – 1.1 μm	

TM	Band 1	0.45 – 0.52 μm	: coastal water mapping, soil vegetation and deciduous/coniferous differentiation
*IFOV =			
30 m	Band 2	0.52 – 0.60 μm	: green reflectance by healthy vegetation
	Band 3	0.63 – 0.69 μm	: chlorophyll absorption for plant species differentiation
	Band 4	0.76 – 0.90 μm	: biomass surveys and water differentiation
	Band 5	1.55 – 1.75 μm	: vegetation moisture measurement; snow/cloud differentiation
	Band 6	2.08 – 2.35 μm	: hydrothermal mapping
	Band 7	10.40 – 12.50 μm	: plant heat stress management and other thermal mapping

*IFOV = instantaneous field of view

See NASA (1981) for further details

SPOT

The second of the future satellites to be described is the French SPOT system which has been conceived and designed by the French National Space Centre at Toulouse and which is being built by French industry in association with Belgian and Swedish partners. SPOT, which is due for launch in 1984, differs significantly from Landsat-D and should prove to be the first serious contender to US dominance in terrestrial remote sensing. Table 5 shows some of the basic characteristics of the twin high resolution or HRV imaging instruments.

The first major characteristic to note is the high multispectral resolution with the option of an even higher panchromatic mode. In the multispectral mode, total Earth coverage is obtained every 26 days compared to every 16 days for Landsat-D. However, this is not as serious as it may at first seem because of the second major characteristic of the SPOT programme, the off-nadir viewing capability. By appropriately selecting the orientation of a pointing mirror, which is controllable from the ground, it will be possible to view any region of interest within a 950 km wide strip centred on the satellite ground track. This pointing capability provides 2 interesting options which are:

1.   An increase in the nominal revisit capability. At 45° latitude it will be possible to observe the same point on the ground on 11 occasions over the 26 days. The way the observations would occur is shown in Figure 1.

2.   There is also the possibility of obtaining stereo pairs from images obtained on concurrent days (Figure 1). In such situations, the ratio between the observation base (or distance between the 2 satellite positions) and the height is 0.5 at a latitude of 45°).

These two capabilities combined with the very high spatial resolution given by the SPOT sensors should provide a valuable new dimension to satellite imagery.

TABLE 5   Characteristics of SPOT HRV imaging instruments

	Multispectral mode	Panchromatic mode
Spectral bands	0.50 - 0.59 µm 0.61 - 0.68 µm 0.79 - 0.89 µm	0.51 - 0.73 m
Ground sampling interval	20 x 20 m	10 x 10 m
No. of pixels per line	3000	6000
Ground swath width (nadir viewing) (per sensor)	60 km	60 km
'Grey levels' recorded	256	256
Image data bit rate	25 mbits/s	25 mbits/s

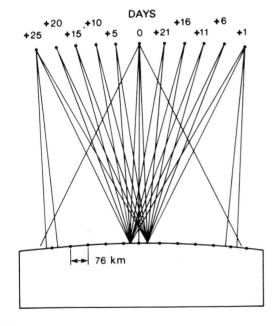

Figure 1   SPOT revisits and stereo-scopic viewing capability

ERS-1

The third of the satellite systems to be described is the ESA ERS-1 satellite. After a number of years of preparation and discussion, the ESA Council decided in October 1981 to undertake the detailed design of a remote sensing satellite (ERS-1) for ocean monitoring applications. The objectives of the satellite mission are both scientific and commercial:

- to develop and promote commercial applications of space data related to a better knowledge of ocean parameters and sea-state conditions;

- to increase scientific understanding of the coastal zones, polar regions and global ocean processes.

The main commercial use of ERS-1 data will be in weather, wind, and wave forecasting for applications sectors such as offshore operations, ship routing and ice surveillance. Scientific value will be in studies of ocean circulation, air-sea interactions, glaciology and climatology.

The baseline payload will comprise essentially active microwave sensors providing an all weather measurement capability. The sensors are:

- a C band *Active Microwave Instrument* (AMI) that combines the functions of a high resolution SAR, a Wave Scatterometer and a Wind Scatterometer;

- a *Radar Altimeter* (RA) primarily for the measurement of significant wave height.

Details of the characteristics of the sensors are given in Table 6.

TABLE 6   ERS-1 payload characteristics

	Performance requirements	
	Parameter	Measurement
1. Active Microwave Instrument		
Synthetic Aperture Radar mode	Resolution	100 x 100 or 30 x 30 m
	Image swath	75 km
Wave mode	Spectral samples	100 m-1000 m in 12 log steps
	Angular samples	30° steps
	Spatial samples	5 km square each 100 km
Wind mode	Resolution	50 km x 50 km
	Wind speed range	4-24 msecs-1
	Accuracy	2 msecs-1 or 10%
	Swath	400 km
2. Radar Altimeter	Altitude	<100 mm
	Wave heights	1-20 m (± 10% or 0.5 m)

In addition to the baseline instruments outlined above, limited capacity is available on the satellite to include a number of scientific instruments to be funded and developed within the framework of national programmes. A key instrument in this additional scientific payload will be the *Along Track Scanning Radiometer* to be developed by the Science and Engineering Research Council (SERC) for measurements of sea surface temperature.

Data from ERS-1 will be transmitted to the ground in real time and through the playback of onboard recorders. The ERS-1 programme will include one data acquisition ground station to be located at Kiruna in northern Sweden. The Kiruna station will receive real time data from the low data rate sensors (Wind and Wave Scatterometers and altimeter) and high data rate SAR sensors, as well as global data from the Wind and Wave Scatterometers and altimeter, stored on board the satellite and played back over the ground station. The raw sensor data will be processed at Kiruna and distributed to users via ground and/or satellite links. Studies are currently underway in the UK to examine how the ERS-1 ground segment should be augmented nationally to meet the requirements of UK users.

MOS-1

The last of the 4 satellite systems to be described is the Japanese Marine Observation Satellite (MOS-1). This is part of an ambitious Earth observation satellite programme comprising both marine and land observation satellites. MOS-1 is the first satellite in this programme, and is scheduled to be launched into a 909 km sun-synchronous orbit in the 1986/7 timeframe. The sensors to be carried on board MOS-1 (Table 7) include both microwave and optical instruments. In addition to the imaging sensors, MOS-1 will also carry a data collection transponder that will permit measurements made by instrumented platforms, as well as details of platform locations, to be relayed via the satellite to a central point.

TABLE 7   Characteristics of sensors to be carried on MOS-1

Sensor/Item	MESSR	VTIR		MSR	
		Visible	Thermal IR	Channel 1	Channel 2
Measurement objective	Sea-surface	Sea-surface temperature		Water content of atmosphere	
Wavelength (μm)	0.51 – 0.59 0.61 – 0.69 0.72 – 0.80 0.80 – 1.1		6 – 7 10.5 – 11.5 11.5 – 12.5		
Frequency (GHz)				23.8	31.4
Geometric Resolution (IFOV in km)	0.05	0.9	2.7	32	23
Radiometric resolution	39 dB	55 dB	$0.5^{o}K$	$1^{o}K$	$1^{o}K$
Swath (km)	100 (1 optical element) x 2	1500	1500	320	320

MESSR = Multispectral Electronic Self-scanning Radiometer
VTIR = Visible and Thermal Infrared Radiometer
MSR = Microwave Scanning Radiometer

It seems clear that the data from the high resolution, visible to near-infrared, sensor (MESSR - see Table 7) will be of interest for land applications, and will provide an interesting point of comparison with Landsat MSS data. Investigations are underway to see if MOS-1 data can be acquired by ground stations in Europe. The choice of X-band frequencies for the satellite-to-earth telemetry links (MESSR and VTIR) will mean, however, that only the more specialized ground stations will be capable of receiving these data.

POLICY ISSUES

In the remainder of this paper, some of the major policy issues which will affect the future of the US and European remote sensing programmes are considered. Perhaps the most significant issue is the question of the commercialization of future missions and the consequent long term continuity of the Landsat series of satellites. In July 1981 it was announced that the Landsat remote sensing programme would end after Landsat-D, unless the private sector had taken over by that time (Marsh 1981).

The present US position represents a substantial hardening of earlier policy which had expressed a longer term commitment to a space borne sensing system and which had designated the National Oceanic and Atmospheric Administration (NOAA) as the operational entity with a longer term policy of transfer to the private sector.

No final decision has yet been made on the eventual US operational remote sensing satellite programme. It is clear, however, that data costs will rise sharply. In addition, there is the possibility that the remote sensing and meteorological missions will be handled together. The strong meteorological influence could well reduce the independence of the other remote sensing element, leaving it very much the poor cousin. If elements of both missions are to be carried on a single space platform, then neither is likely to be optimum.

ESA

The ESA situation is perhaps even more complicated both because of the stage reached in defining the future programme and because it involves 12 countries (including Canada) with very different priorities. What is clear is that the land satellite option debated within ESA for several years has become more distant as the French SPOT programme has become more certain. Whilst a number of countries, including the UK, have stressed the need for the first oceanographic mission to be seen in the context of a comprehensive remote sensing programme, incorporating land and climatological missions, the prospect of a land mission before 1990 now seems remote.

The French position in the European space arena is becoming - or perhaps has become - dominant. France is expected to contribute significantly to the cost of the ESA ERS-1 mission, in addition to developing the national SPOT programme into an operational 10 year series of land observation satellites. The UK contribution to the ERS-1 programme is likely to be about 13% and our national programme is only a fraction of that of the French. However, the UK is currently considering its involvement in ERS-1, and in particular the need for a related national remote sensing programme to prepare for ERS-1 exploitation. As part of this national programme, the Natural Environment Research Council (NERC) and SERC are also considering the level and direction of their research programmes for the next few years. It is to be hoped that some increase in remote sensing directed effort will be achieved as a result of these UK initiations.

In addition, it should be stressed that Japan and Canada are also now active in the remote sensing area and that the Japanese involvement and influence are likely to grow dramatically in the next 10 years. The Canadians are putting a special effort into microwave remote sensing and especially the role of imaging radars for ice and ocean surveillance.

CONCLUSIONS

This paper has by its nature touched briefly on many issues, each of which could have justified a longer discussion in its own right. Even in this abbreviated fashion, we have not discussed adequately the issues of the potential explosion in the quantity of data and the relevant developments in image processing hardware and software. What is clear, however, is that the success of Landsat, Seasat and other satellite missions is such that, even with the current serious economic depression, the collection of Earth observation data from satellites is likely to increase rapidly. The improvement in spatial, spectral and temporal resolution plus the SPOT stereoscopic capability will result in many new and potentially powerful applications of space data leading to the introduction of operational systems in the 1990s.

SUMMARY

Since 1972, the United States Landsat series of satellites has provided a global and repetitive basis, medium resolution multispectral data. A parallel development in image analysis hardware and in the related computer software has led to the experimental use of Landsat data over a wide range of environmental applications. A new generation of environmental satellites will be launched in the next decade which will provide optically sensed data with greatly improved spatial and spectral resolution. The first of these satellites, Landsat-D, will be launched mid-1982 and this will be followed by the French SPOT satellite, with a 10 m resolution and stereoscopic capability, in 1984. In addition, a number of microwave sensors, including an imaging radar, are scheduled to be flown by ESA from 1987 onwards, and there are other USA, Japanese and Indian missions planned.

REFERENCES

MARSH, A.K. 1981. Landsat extension to rest on private sector support. *Aviat. Week Space Technol.*, 115, 26-27.
NATIONAL AERONAUTICS AND SPACE ADMINISTRATION. 1981. *Applications notice for participation in the Landsat-D image data quality analysis program.* Houston, Texas: NASA.